The DIVINE PRINCIPLES

of *Mothering*

The DIVINE

PRINCIPLES

of *Mothering*

JANICE GERBER NIELSON

CFI
Springville, Utah

This is not an official publication of The Church of Jesus Christ of Latter-day Saints. The opinions and views expressed herein belong solely to the author and do not necessarily represent the opinions or views of Cedar Fort, Inc. Permission for the use of sources, graphics, and photos is also solely the responsibility of the author.

ISBN 13: 978-1-59955-247-7

Published by CFI, an imprint of Cedar Fort, Inc., 2373 W. 700 S., Springville, UT 84663
Distributed by Cedar Fort, Inc., www.cedarfort.com

LIBRARY OF CONGRESS CATALOGING-IN-PUBLICATION DATA

Nielson, Janice Gerber, 1945-
The Divine Principles of Mothering / Janice Gerber Nielson.
p. cm.
ISBN 978-1-59955-247-7 (alk. paper)
1. Motherhood—Religious aspects—Christianity. 2. Mothers—Religious life. I. Title.

BV4529.18.N54 2009
248.8'431--dc22

2008043668

Cover design by Nicole Williams
Cover design © 2009 by Lyle Mortimer
Edited and typeset by Heidi Doxey

Printed in the United States of America

10 9 8 7 6 5 4 3 2 1

Printed on acid-free paper

Dedication

This book is dedicated to the mothers in Zion who care so deeply for their children and who work so devotedly for their children's eternal welfare.

Contents

Acknowledgments

I owe a debt of gratitude to the many LDS mothers who participated with integrity and diligence in my research projects; to my professors who informed and guided me; and to the great women in my life I have been privileged to associate with and who have mentored and inspired me.

This book, and the precepts and illustrations upon which it is based, would not have been possible without my own family. My husband and children have brought joy and fulfillment to my experience in mothering.

Chapter One

Eternal Principles
of Mothering

This is both a personal and, I believe, a universal story about mothering. While most of my real-life experiences as a mother are representative of other mothers, I have a purpose in giving this account. Through a lifetime of study, practice, and prayer, I have come to recognize and appreciate the eternal principles that underlie all good mothering, and hope to reverently bring those timeless principles to our attention. Before doing that, however, I would like to briefly explain my perspective on mothering by describing how study, practice, and prayer have played such a large part in my story.

I began studying the role of a mother when my husband, Corrin, and I were expecting our first child. As I look back I realize I should have given this topic considerably more attention prior to that time. I mistakenly assumed it could not be too difficult to be a mother since most women at some point in their lives take upon themselves the bearing and rearing of children. I felt my life was unfolding in a fairly predictable way. My easy assumptions were shattered when our small infant daughter, Carrie, lived only eight hours. She was born, lived, and died on Mother's Day that year, and my husband and I grieved as our little daughter with the strawberry-blonde curls was with us for such a brief time. I realized that the blessing of children in our lives is a gift, not a given.

We were grateful when we found that I was again expecting a baby, and I was now preparing and learning in earnest. Through those early

1

years, I studied pregnancy and childbirth, and took infancy and child development classes. I had a genuine desire to care for my children in the best possible way and I needed to know how to do so. Over time I continued to fit a class into my busy schedule whenever the demands of a growing family permitted. However, because the care of a large family consumed so much of my time, it was not until many years later that I completed a PhD in psychology. While the degree was in social/personality psychology, developmental psychology comprised a significant portion of my interest and work, providing me with a wealth of information and many relevant ideas to ponder. Though I recognized and appreciated the valid and scientifically-based research that illuminates the study of behavior, there were incorrect or partially correct suppositions that needed to be sorted through as well. I scrutinized every theory I encountered to see how it explained the question, "What makes a person happy?" As I contemplated the answer given by each theorist I learned to sort truth from error. Therefore, though I found secular learning to be valuable in very real and practical terms, it was also of great benefit in that it allowed me to compare and contrast the ideas of theorists and professional experts with Gospel truths and with my own experiences rearing a family.

In addition to my pursuit of a secular education, I have experienced—in considerable depth and breadth—the reality of being a mother. During the nineteen years after we buried our firstborn we had eleven more children. Whether it was teaching a young child how to use a spoon or teaching a teenager how to drive a car, I practiced it eleven times. I had my own ready-made "living laboratory" of growing, developing children. I am quite certain our children readily recall my frequent statement, "I have an idea," and how we would troop upstairs to the living room for an impromptu meeting where we would make plans to improve some detail of our lives. Today, many of the children are married with families of their own while others are still single and living at home part-time; the living, learning, and loving continues.

The third component that explains my perspective is prayer. Like most mothers I cannot count how many times I have fallen to my knees in prayer, needing wisdom beyond my own. I was frequently confused as I sorted through the advice of experts in the field, the counsel of other mothers, and my own experiences. It took prayerful consideration in order to feel the peace that comes when the correct conclusion is reached or the right decision is made. I wish I could say I had, through study, trial-and-error, and prayer, received all the answers. Instead, I am more convinced than ever that the art of mothering will be perfected in the eternities. We mothers, like our children, are works in progress.

As I endeavored to be a nurturing mother, to study all I could find concerning the skills related to mothering, and to seek for divine help, there emerged to my view those principles that were enduring, that would guide and center mothering. I realized that when we shape our mothering to reflect these truths we tread on secure ground. We can confidently love and guide our children as we learn to parent the same way our Father in Heaven parents us. This great underlying reality will become clearer as we speak of these timeless truths.

However, if the principles of which we speak are eternal, it follows that they must apply to all mothers; we wonder how this can be so when the face of mothering changes from place to place and from time to time. Some expressions of mothering may appear very different from those with which we are familiar. Times do change and the circumstances in which mothers find themselves change with them. Certainly, Mother Eve had no requirements to attend PTA conferences or transport her offspring to games, school events, and after-school activities; and even though our grandmothers worked hard to meet the daily demands of rearing children, the obligations came in different ways than we experience today.

Not only do the settings and requirements of mothering differ from generation to generation, but circumstances worldwide vary remarkably—even in this day and age. My husband and I taught for the Church at universities in China for several years. During our daily cross-campus walks to class I was particularly fascinated watching grandmothers gathered together around an on-campus fountain, socializing with one another as each "mothered" her sole young grandbaby. Equally fascinating were my observations of each well-bundled baby in split-bottomed pants busily discovering his world. I came to learn that, in China, by using a multi-generational approach to "mothering," the child's father and mother could both work to provide for the three generations of their household. If we were to survey a variety of cultures, from a one-child-policy in China to nomadic families in Africa, we would observe the varied faces of mothering.

Even in highly developed countries, broadly differing circumstances are apparent. Undoubtedly, the challenges of rearing a family in a crowded tenement within a large city are much different from those in a more rural setting. How society views motherhood changes over time as well. The expectations, perceptions, and values regarding the family are in flux on many fronts.

Given such diverse descriptions it may seem daunting to identify abiding principles of mothering that remain true in every age and setting. Yet, there are essential components of mothering so fundamental to raising happy, productive children, that they transcend time, surroundings, and cultures. It is the intent of this work to look carefully at the foundational principles of all good mothering. Of course, circumstances will not always permit the full expression of these basic tenets, but if we know them we can then apply them to the fullest extent possible. This will also allow us to compensate for many environmental factors we are not able to change. The effort to come closer to, or approximate the ideal will yield profound results, and we will be rewarded as good mothering becomes great mothering. These universal requirements are so essential to the well-being of a child that they are acknowledged by both divine and secular authority. It is my desire to increase the awareness of these principles and to relate some of the things I have learned about applying such truths. Illustrations of real successes and failures may serve as food for thought for other mothers as they work to create the world which will shape their children.

This is not a "how-to" manual where we concern ourselves with the methodologies related to child care. Any method for handling a developmental task usually has both positive and negative aspects. For example, there are many approaches to toilet training. I was interested while visiting in Europe to see a young mother place her small daughter in a combination high chair/potty chair for her meal. I wondered about the hygiene and the pleasantness of having food and its waste product so near one another. On the other hand, the timing makes sense since peristalsis of the colon is stimulated when a new meal reaches the stomach. Consider, as well, the split-bottom pants of those rosy-cheeked Chinese babies. Permitting a diaperless or more natural approach means the immediate environment is subjected to some unpleasant smells and residues. Yet, the global environment is better off without millions of disposable diapers decomposing very slowly in landfills. So there are supporters and detractors for every method, and we can get bogged down in inconclusive debates when focusing on competing techniques or methodologies.

However, it is not to say that the methods we choose in training children have no importance. Knowing what I do about child development

I certainly think some procedures are more effective than others. I used to discuss with my mother my reasons for delaying the toilet training of a small son or daughter. I knew the process would go more smoothly if I waited until signs of readiness became apparent in the young child. She, having been reared in another culture, believed babies should be trained by the time they were one year old. I knew Mother was caring and dedicated, yet I remained unconvinced of the advisability of that approach and remembered hearing of a time when customs officials at a port-of-entry took pity on my mother because of a toilet-training mishap on my part. I was a very young toddler at the time and had my "accident" on the sleeve of Mother's good fur coat, where she was carrying me with one arm while at the same time holding onto the hand of my three-year-old sister with the other. The customs officials saw the situation and waved her past the checkpoints. At eighteen months old, according to Mother's system, I should have already been trained for six months, and, of course, eventually I was. Most systems work, because, for the most part, we all end up potty-trained. Of more consequence than the actual toilet training is how gently we accomplish the task, and how the small child feels about him or herself when we are done. The central point is that children can grow up to be happy, well-adjusted adults, using many child-rearing techniques, if the essential eternal principles described in this work are observed.

Volumes have been written about mothers and mothering. In order to draw attention to the most vital principles of mothering it is necessary to leave untouched some helpful guidelines which might pertain to this discussion and focus, instead, on three principles which comprise the essence of divine mothering; namely, love, security, and guidance. It is my conviction that most, if not all, true applications of mothering can be included within these three core principles. When we gain a true understanding of these three imperatives we can use them as the measure by which we judge the efficacy, value, and long-term implications of every other aspect of our mothering. Love, security, and guidance are essential to our success.

Chapter Two

LOVE AS THE FOUNDATION OF MOTHERING

There would be few women who would not immediately list love among the attributes essential for good mothering—very likely ranking it first. It feels intuitive, perhaps God-given. Indeed, it is difficult to imagine children growing into full, resplendent manhood or womanhood who have not been nurtured with love by someone important to them in their formative years. President Gordon B. Hinckley tells us, "Children need sunlight. They need happiness. They need love and nurture. They need kindness and refreshment and affection. Every home, regardless of the cost of the house, can provide an environment of love which will be an environment of salvation."[1] Because of the ascendancy of love among the qualities of a good mother it is especially important to get this one right, and to understand how it guides and impacts every other principle about which we shall speak.

Though the love of a mother is natural and pure, mothers are not. We are not omniscient, unsullied by temptation, or disciplined in our every action. We are like everyone else here on Earth—getting a lot right, stumbling quite often, learning, growing, making mistakes, and moving forward. That is why Mother's Day may at times leave us feeling just a little defeated. Motherhood is so important we really should be perfect at it, yet we are not. Nevertheless, we sense that putting our best efforts into this undertaking will be worth it, and we are willing to learn and grow, to work hard, and to sacrifice for the good of our children.

Other-Centeredness

As a graduate student my research focused on altruism; that is, helping behaviors. I performed an extensive literature review of the work already completed on the subject. Later, when I conducted the field research for both my master's thesis and doctoral dissertation, I examined actual acts of service performed by LDS mothers. Some of the results of that intensive study are relevant to this work.

Though the acts of service were important and usually successful in bringing about the intended relief, the reason an individual performed the helping behavior was far more interesting and pertinent. I found that if the helper (the mother) was focused on the person she was assisting, she was empathic and caring, selfless in her service, and felt joy and fulfillment. If the same helping behaviors were performed when the mother was focused on herself, rather than on the one in need, the results were far different.

Let me give a hypothetical example to make this point. In this illustration a mother readies her young daughters for church by dressing them in lovely matching outfits she has sewn herself. Knowing the effort she has made for her girls, what might we surmise about this mother? One possible motive might be that the mother loves these little girls and wants them to feel good and confident about themselves. She expects her efforts may also help the children to be more reverent in their worship. As the mother builds and strengthens her daughters, she is other-centered in her motivations. She is thinking of her girls and not of herself.

Contrariwise, perhaps this act of service is really about the mother. Of course, she loves the girls, but she has an image she wishes to uphold. She needs to look as though she has things put together; maybe that she is even quite talented. She needs validation from others. In this instance, the focus shifts from the children to the mother and is no longer other-centered.

Another possible explanation for this mother's actions is that sewing beautiful and appropriate clothing for her children reflects the way she was trained. She sees such actions as a duty or a moral imperative. She does not want to feel guilty by not doing it. Her need to be guilt-free makes this, once again, about her, and thus self-centered.

She may even be constructing what psychologists term a social exchange relationship; wherein she makes an effort to dress her children especially well, and in exchange she expects certain things from her children. Essentially, the children unintentionally assume an obligation either to perform certain behaviors in the present, or to "owe" their mother after they are grown.

Yet, another possibility is that the mother has made a master list of all the things she should do, and this service to her daughters is on the list. It is important to her because she is striving for perfection. But it is *her* need for perfection. Again, the focus is on the mother rather than on her young daughters and can no longer be considered other-centered.

This hypothetical story reveals that for any one behavior there can be many reasons for performing that particular action. If the focus is on the one being helped, the motivation is other-centered. If it is for other reasons, such as the need to look good, to live without feelings of guilt, or to obligate another, the focus changes and becomes a self-centered motivation.

Most of the selfish motivations listed above may make sense to us, but what about the desire to seek for our own perfection? How can working toward perfection be wrong? Of course, it is not wrong to seek to be perfect; indeed, we are commanded to do so. It is more a matter of how we are to go about it, and for that guidance we look to our Savior.

Jesus Christ, Himself, has told us that it is only by losing ourselves in His work that we can be saved. "He that findeth his life shall lose it: and he that loseth his life for my sake shall find it" (Matthew 11:39). Elder Gordon B. Hinckley, while a member of the Twelve, explained these words further: "These words have something more than a cold theological meaning. They are a statement of a law of life—that as we lose ourselves in a great cause we find ourselves—and there is no greater cause than that of the Master."[2] By forgetting ourselves and focusing on the needs of others we grow into perfection and ensure our own salvation.

All of the great scriptures on charity make this assertion plain. "Let all your things be done with charity" (1 Corinthians 16:14). If we do everything right and perform every act of service we are capable of, but do so selfishly, without charity, and without the pure love of Christ, our efforts are in vain. Whenever we as mothers do the right thing for the wrong reason we diminish the experience. Motive is everything. Whether our reasons for service are selfish or selfless is everything. If we worry about our image, talents, or expectations; our rewards and recognitions; our need for validation; or our need to avoid censure or guilt; we are acting selfishly. The "great cause" we as mothers want to lose ourselves in is the rearing of a righteous generation. Only when we set our own interests aside and focus on the well-being of our children does motherly love qualify as being one of those eternal principles of which we speak.

Does being other-centered mean, then, that we should take no thought for ourselves? Do we not matter? The answer is that we most definitely do matter. It is much more difficult to be a good mother if we are tired, unwell, distracted, or bored. It is imperative that we see to our needs for healthy food, appropriate exercise, learning and intellectual stimulation, rest and relaxation, enjoying social and interpersonal relationships, peaceful contemplation and spiritual renewal, and a myriad of other things that refresh and replenish us.

The critical question is not whether we should take care of ourselves, rather, why we should do so. If we foresee that taking good care of ourselves and being happy enables us to serve others better, we have achieved a critical understanding. In the ultimate sense, our concern should be our serviceability. We are on this earth not only to learn, grow, and be tested, but to have joy. The Lord wants us to appreciate the beauties of this earth, to enjoy one another, and to experience anticipation, excitement, and fulfillment. However, we are also expected to do all we can to increase our energy and lengthen our days, and prepare ourselves as well as we are able, in order that our contributions can be greater both in number and meaningfulness. Life's most profound joys will be experienced as we do so. Such preparation frees a mother to focus on her children and feel the joy that results from her selflessness.

I remember one summer after school let out, my eldest daughter, now married and with her own family, considered the lazy, warm months ahead and decided she wanted her children to use some of their free time in a constructive way. So she developed a number of teaching units that she felt would be fun to undertake. One of those modules was the study of birds. Together, she and the children read and researched the subject, checked out videos about birds from the library, and watched bird eggs hatch in the backyard. During one of my visits, the children enthusiastically showed me the pictures of birds they had attached to the wall around the dining room window. The pictures enabled them to analyze the markings and identify the birds that came to feed at the three bird feeders they had hung in the trees outside the window. The children were very excited and knowledgeable about birds when they completed the last segment of the unit by going on a field trip to the Tracy Aviary in Salt Lake City.

Did it take effort to make a summer like that happen? Without a doubt! It might have been tempting for this mother to catch up on some easy reading and let the days go by. But, we are talking about joy here. What enjoyment she and the kids had doing these things together! My daughter chose to focus on her children, and they knew they mattered. Without my needing to ask her, I could see she was a happy mother. Love was really the subject of that summer. Learning all about birds was just a fun bonus.

Achieving Balance

Though successful mothering requires that we consider the well-being of both mother and child, the appropriate balance between the two may not always be clear. We may comprehend the vision of selfless mothering and seek earnestly to care for our children, yet realize we must meet our own needs for stimulation, good health, beauty, and so forth, if we are to be successful in our stewardship. It may not be easy to know the correct balance between the two.

By way of illustration, I recall one afternoon the children trudged up the long hill from the bus stop and, as usual, plopped all their assorted books and paraphernalia on the kitchen counter as they entered the house. I noticed one of the teenagers had the book, *Jurassic Park*, on his stack and I picked it up out of curiosity. At the time, there was a lot of buzz about the movie by the same title, but I had not yet seen it. Having a weakness for books, in short order I began to read and was hooked. I could not easily put it down and had to tear myself away to see to dinner; then it was back to the book. That was how the evening passed as I seesawed between taking care of my responsibilities and reading the book. I felt relief when everyone was finally settled for the night and I could read without interruption. I finished the book about four o'clock in the wee hours of the morning, knowing that I would be dragging the following day. I also knew the toddlers and preschoolers would be well-rested, and that all the demands of a full day lay ahead.

I now reflect on that experience and question my choice at the time. Fortunately, I seldom did such rash things. And I wonder . . . did I need an "escape" in my life just then? Was I wearying, perhaps not meeting my need to have new things to think about? Was I out of balance in some way, or was it something much more simple?—I just wanted to read that book!

I certainly recognized days when I spent time thinking about myself, or more particularly the concerns related to me. I may have been bothered that I was getting out-of-shape, resentful that I was too far away to see my parents as much as I would have liked, disappointed that I could not go to a ward social because some of the children were not well, or any number of other things. Mothers are not exempt from such yearnings. However, I also came to recognize that the days when I got out of bed and focused on the needs of my children, wanting them to be happy, desiring to provide them a good balance between stimulating learning activities and sweet, peaceful times together, were my happy days. I loved it when I created such a day! Admittedly, it may not always be easy for us to tell in advance what our righteous wants and needs are and how we can balance them with our children's wants and needs. I have come to believe that it may take some prayerful thought to discover them.

Yet, another related feature about love should be understood. Women who are mothers also play many other roles. Mothers are usually, but not always, married during much or all of the child-rearing years. We love, and are in love with, that man who stands by our side and carries his own heavy load in the care of the family. How are we to nurture this treasured relationship while providing for the many needs of a growing family? I think of the days when my husband was in college and working on his advanced degrees, and I did the editing and typing of his many research papers. I often typed late into the night. In order to meet the looming deadlines the needs of my small children sometimes had to be edited as well. Necessary chores had to be swiftly completed and less essential matters put off until a later time. I had to repeatedly remind myself that people matter more than things, as the living room began looking a little too well-lived-in as the children played while I typed. Though we tried to make certain security and love were ever present, even the lingering cuddles sometimes had to be temporarily condensed when a more pressing issue was addressed.

The question arises: what is the effect on children when a mother's focus broadens to include other people? The answer: it depends. It depends on how old the children are, how much they understand, how long the attention is divided, what other caring persons surround them, and for what reason the mother is less accessible. We will consider issues of attention and security in a later chapter, but an important thought regarding the principle of love needs to be addressed in the present context.

Just as our ultimate goal as mothers is to lose ourselves in the service of others, the same purpose exists for every person, male or female—including our children. As we model a wide variety of helping behaviors our children learn how to care for others, how to look beyond their own interests, and they are better positioned to grow into service-minded individuals. If we are successful in helping them become other-centered rather than self-centered we have done a great deal to ensure their happiness.

One of the challenges that came to our family is illustrative of this topic. As my own mother aged and grew increasingly dependent my siblings and I struggled to meet her needs. Of course, we loved her and wanted to care for her properly. During the times she lived with our family we had opportunities to experience both the costs and rewards of service. Because our family was so large our living space was never as adequate as we would have liked. The girls jostled for closet space, and we had double-wide bunk beds made to accommodate the boys. When Mother came to us she needed to have a bedroom to herself because of her special requirements. Losing a bedroom really put us in tight quarters. I used to lie awake nights trying to figure out how to meet each person's needs. I knew it was important to provide a modicum of personal space and privacy for each child, and I worked to make that happen, but I understood that Mother's dependency put her needs before those of the children.

I realized that this was a time of testing and growth for both the children and me, and that the children could be taught the importance of sacrificing for a greater good. As it turned out we all learned a lot. Part of my study of altruism dealt with research pertaining to the role of a caretaker. I recognized myself as being one of those in the "sandwich" generation—taking care of the generations on either side of me—and I could relate to the stresses they described in the various studies. I felt them. I strained to get it right and experienced mixed emotions as I sorted through what I needed to do each day. I believe the children, too, are better people for having made room for their grandmother in their home, their thoughts, and their hearts, during her time of need.

In addition to family there are many other people within the circle of a woman's reach who may command time and attention. Whether it is paid employment, educational endeavors, volunteer work, neighborly watchcare, socializing time with friends, church callings, or any one of a number of other possible associations, a woman's contacts are many. Some women benefit humanity on a larger scale, maybe contributing their talents to the sciences or arts or education. They may be paid or unpaid for their efforts in these many arenas, but each interaction becomes a decision point for the mother of children: how do I prioritize my time and attention so that my children's physical, emotional, social, mental, and spiritual needs are well met?

To direct our thinking here, it might be well to ask some additional questions: Are there any other pursuits more important than mothering? If so, what would they be? Is it an "either/or" proposition anyway? Can we mothers succeed in multiple purposes? When we are required to choose between a focus on our children and attending to other matters, how do we make that decision? These are difficult questions that every mother will have to contemplate more times that she can count. I believe we mothers can resolve such dilemmas if we establish and adhere to some general guidelines.

First, when we look at the time we spend achieving and contributing to the world around us we feel a sense of satisfaction, especially if our efforts are meritorious. Any worthy purpose should be applauded if (and it is a very big "if") it has not come at the expense of the family. We are counseled by a prophet of God, "No other success can compensate for failure in the home."[3] So our first guideline is to be sure our homes rank before all worldly pursuits, whether those pursuits are other-centered or not. Working mothers have a unique challenge in this context and we shall return to that subject in a later chapter.

Second, because nurturing and caring for family members rarely takes all of a mother's time, opportunities for a woman to contribute her time and talents to worthy endeavors are plentiful. Caring for the less fortunate; rendering aid and comfort wherever it is needed; serving devotedly in church callings; considering the welfare of neighbors and friends; and sharing expertise, education, and talents for the betterment and enlightenment of our society, are not only noble pursuits but necessary ones. The world needs its women, inside the home and out.

Third, wisdom is required to know which of all competing needs are the most urgent in any single circumstance. It is often a fine line we mothers try to decipher while juggling the many demands of our everyday lives. A Relief Society president may need to skip her son's game or her daughter's recital as she comforts a new widow in the ward. A mother may awaken a small child out of a sound sleep in order to transport a friend to the hospital. The fun lesson and treat planned for home evening may need to be postponed as the entire family helps clean up a neighbor's flooded basement. It is good for children to realize their needs are not the only needs under consideration.

A mother of a large family told me of an instance when she had arranged to use church facilities for a family event because the activities planned required more space than her home provided. She had made plans well in advance and had gone to a lot of effort to get everything prepared. When she and her children arrived at the church to set up they learned that a funeral was being held in the building, and that they would not be able to have the event in the way they had planned and would need to make some adjustments. She waved aside the apologies given, replying that the funeral was more important, and they would make out some other way. Even though they were all disappointed, this mother made a concerted effort to teach her children the value of recognizing priorities, and demonstrated to her children by her attitude that some needs are more important than others.

Clearly, the question is not always whether to serve, but whom we should serve. I have learned in my years of mothering to follow this wise counsel, which seems to help in making these tough decisions: do the right thing in the moment. This assumes that at any given decision point in our lives there is an optimal way of proceeding. There is no way of our knowing in advance what the particulars or context of any moment in time will be. The only thing we can decide beforehand is that we will try to do the right thing. Therefore, as we are faced with the competing needs of others we need to pause and ask ourselves: what is the right thing to do in this moment? The mother who graciously put the unexpected funeral ahead of her own plans exemplified this concept.

Often we will know the correct choice as we pause at one of those decision-points; other times the situation may be more complex and we may experience a stupor of thought as to the best way to proceed. When our own wisdom and experience are not sufficient, we can look to a higher source for answers. There may be many studied opinions, theories, and scientific investigations worthy of our consideration, but truth is most surely uncovered by going to its source. The Prophet Joseph Smith appealed to this source after reading this scripture: "If any of you lack wisdom, let him ask of God, that giveth to all men liberally, and upbraideth not; and it shall be given him" (James 1:5). That invitation is extended to all of us. We can receive revelation in the very moment we need it, and can thereby serve our children and others better.

May I reveal how I came to believe so strongly in inspiration? When I was a young mother with small children, I felt a convergence of scriptural truths as a number of scriptures and ideas came into my mind at about the same time. First, I came to understand that each of us is allowed to seek for spiritual gifts; indeed, not just allowed, but counseled to seek for gifts that would strengthen us and make us more useful. "And again I would exhort you that ye would come unto Christ, and lay hold upon every good gift, and touch not the evil gift, nor the unclean thing" (Moroni 10:30).

Second, I thought of King Solomon who spoke with the Lord near the beginning of his reign: "In that night did God appear unto Solomon, and said unto him, Ask what I shall give thee" (2 Chronicles 1:7). In his now famous reply, Solomon said, "Give unto me wisdom and knowledge, that I may go out and come in before this people: for who can judge this thy people, that is so great?" (2 Chronicles 1:10). Notice the motive for King Solomon's request; it was for the good of those he ruled, and not for any self-interest. His demonstration of selflessness was acknowledged by the Lord.

> And God said to Solomon, because this was in thine heart; and thou hast not asked riches, wealth, or honour, nor the life of thine enemies, neither yet has asked long life; but has asked wisdom and knowledge for thyself, that thou mayest judge my people, over whom I have made thee king: wisdom and knowledge is granted unto thee; and I will give thee riches, and wealth, and honour, such as none of the kings have had that have been before thee, neither shall there any after thee have the like" (2 Chronicles 1:11–12).

I thought for a long time about the selfless request Solomon made for wisdom.

Third, as I was contemplating the Lord's interaction with Solomon, I was also reading the *Discourses of Brigham Young.* There I noted how all of us are granted the right to revelation in our lives. Particularly was I drawn to this passage: "It is the right of the mother who labors in the kitchen with her little prattling children around, to enjoy the Spirit of Christ, and to know her duty with regard to her children."[4]

As I pondered these ideas I asked myself what gift I would choose were the Lord to grant me the desire of my heart. I realized it would be similar to the wisdom for which Solomon sought. Though I had no need of wisdom to judge thousands, because of my mothering stewardship I did need great wisdom in rearing my children. Having become secure in the knowledge that mothers have the right to the spirit in caring for their children, I began to make that my heartfelt plea from that time forth. Over many years I prayed regularly for that special wisdom, and on many occasions I received it. I have come to feel and trust that directing spirit.

I believe as we practice and put forth effort we will get better at weighing these decisions of whom to serve (and when and how). Knowledge and experience will help us, but our greatest source of help will come from within as the soft impressions of the Spirit nudge us in the right direction. "Every good gift and every perfect gift is from above, and cometh down from the Father of lights, with whom is no variableness, neither shadow of turning" (James 1:17). We ponder and analyze using our experience, reason, and learning (as the Lord desires us to do), but we also listen and feel, and have faith that our prayers to know what is right will be answered.

What Love Is Not

An important part of this discussion about love is to note what it is not. It is not giving children everything they want. This axiom of child rearing is seemingly obvious, yet quite problematic in implementation. Even if we have caught the vision of focusing on the needs of the child, distinguishing needs from wants can present difficulties for parents. To children all wants are needs, and they often expect Mother to supply both. Since we know a child can become demanding, even spoiled, if all wants are supplied, parental experience and maturity are often required to balance wants and needs.

Moreover, we mothers must exercise care that we do for our children only those things they cannot do for themselves; and must require them to do whatever they are capable of doing. We can cripple their progress with too much hovering, and we can undermine their confidence if we require more than they are comfortable doing. Ideally, we should expect the acquisition and performance of a new skill when a child is developmentally ready and physically capable of performing the task. Timing is everything here, and this is where mothering is more an art than a science. We will consider the basics of training children in a later chapter.

In the context of love we should choose to do for our children those things which will bring them success and happiness in the long run, and curtail the things which may bring momentary pleasure but will not serve them well over time. The scriptures help us recognize that this is the way our Heavenly Father parents us. Never should we reward poor behavior, for if we do so we only bring about an increase in the unwanted conduct. For example, if a child pleads for a sweet treat at the grocery store and succeeds in wearing down Mom by whining or throwing tantrums, such manipulative behaviors will increase. We should never facilitate behavior which is counterproductive to the best interest of the child, even when giving in brings the child momentary happiness and the mother temporary peace. It is natural to want our children to love us, and even to like us, but mothering is not about popularity. We will make many unpopular decisions over the course of our parenting. At times we may even feel uncomfortable ourselves when we do so; it may be inconvenient or difficult to remain firm in our decisions when we are in embarrassing or rushed circumstances. Nevertheless, when we know the answer should be "no," we must have the fortitude to give that answer, because that is what is ultimately right for our child.

Love with a Light Touch

As we serve with love it helps to keep the tone light. Lightness and love go together. These words connote cheerfulness, optimism, and hope. Rearing children with humor and lightheartedness is a gift mothers can give them. Let me give an example. I vividly recall a time when my first four daughters were small and all of them were crying at the same time. I quickly determined nothing was seriously wrong with any of them; rather, each was irritable for various trivial reasons. I spontaneously addressed the issue something like this: "My, my, what is all this about? If you're all going to cry we ought to at least do a good job of it. So, I will be the 'conductor' and you girls will be the 'criers.' Try to cry your very best." Then I stood up in front of them and waved my arm, leading them in their crying, and encouraging them when they started to slow down. "Kathryn, you're fading a bit. . . . A little louder, Natalie. . . . No, no. No laughing! Remember, this is a crying chorus." It was not long before my "criers" became "gigglers," and their grumpiness melted away. My daughters' easy transition from upset to cheerful was so dramatic it attested to me the power of the light touch in child rearing. A lighter touch, or a good sense of humor, can often maintain or restore the loving atmosphere we all desire in our homes. The good news here is that we can train ourselves and our children to see the funny parts of life, and to use humor effectively to soften feelings and change the home climate. Let me illustrate another way I tried to lighten the mood while still accomplishing my goal of getting the children up in the morning—a process which grew increasingly unpopular with them the older they became. I had a variety of cheerful little songs I sang to them. One of those short tunes I sang to them was one I had been exposed to while growing up in Provo. The first line was a jaunty, "Rise and shout, the Nielson's are out." Later, when we moved for one year to Provo where I could spend full time on my graduate work, we were living in the "tree streets" near BYU. One morning, my middle-school-age boys could hear the BYU marching band practicing on the field below us and came hurrying to find me. "They're playing our song!" they exclaimed. They did not know I had sort of adapted the Cougar Fight Song for my own purposes.

As counterpoint to my methods, my husband generally awakened the children by clapping his hands loudly and monotonously until they stirred. It was an irritant they could not ignore. They hated it! We still tease him about it, and he still attests to its effectiveness. (I think it may be a guy thing.) Both methods may work, but for mothers, I side with gentler, cheerier ways.

Meaningful words such as light, truth, love, and happiness are often grouped together. We will better achieve a feeling of love in our homes if we lighten the tone, be quick to laugh, and be positive as we move through the day, helping our children to see the humor in situations and to look for silver linings everywhere.

Notes

1. Gordon B. Hinckley, "Save the Children," *Ensign*, Nov. 1994, 54.
2. Gordon B. Hinckley, Conference Report, Apr. 1966, 87.
3. David O. McKay, *Improvement Era*, June 1964, 445.
4. *Discourses of Brigham Young*, sel. John A. Widtsoe, (Salt Lake City: Deseret Book, 1946), 200.

Chapter Three

Security Provides the Safety to Grow

It would be difficult to overrate the importance of security in family life. Along with love and guidance, it is a necessary component in rearing happy and healthy children. A secure childhood gives a small son or daughter permission to grow and to thrive. We may know of many instances, particularly in times of war or natural disasters, where children come through perilous experiences intact, both physically and emotionally. For countless others, such trauma is insurmountable. Safety is a universal human need.

Beyond the obvious requirement to protect life and limb, there are other questions of security—some much more subtle. Do children feel free to explore their environment, or are they constrained by fearfulness? Does anxiety impede their growth? Do they see the world as a friendly place, or a scary unknown? What kind of adults will insecure children become? These are all important questions to ask and answer as we try to do the right thing for our children. There are two essentials relating to security that need to be addressed: predictability and accessibility. We will examine these in some depth, but first I would like to comment on a third aspect which can be explained in a few paragraphs, and serves primarily as a caution to parents.

Children need to be protected from themselves. This does not mean keeping them from physically hurting themselves—although that is important—rather, that we protect them from their own emotions.

Achieving emotional maturity is a developmental issue, and instruction and training cannot hurry it much beyond its physiological parameters. Occasionally a child's emotional outburst will escalate out of control, and that scares him or her. Not knowing how to stop or manage these runaway passions, they rely on those with cooler, more mature heads to step in. It is as though we are saying, "You don't have to worry; I won't let you go too far."

Even teenagers have not yet achieved full developmental control of their emotions (though they usually think they have). When they become too impassioned, it is a good time to exercise your cool and tone down or soften the discourse. Usually, with some time and after some reflection, the adolescent will have thought things through and be able to think more dispassionately. We play for time here, not immediate resolution of the matter.

The caution for mothers, then, is to be the adult in the best sense of the word. We, as adults, can control our emotions and it is vital that we do so. Our maturity and experience can be used to smooth and guide the emotions in our children, and thereby give them a much-needed sense of security.

Predictability

Let me begin this section by giving you an extreme hypothetical scenario. I do this in order to pointedly illustrate the importance of predictability in a child's life. Let us suppose that in a certain family, whenever the father returns home his wife and son never know what kind of mood he will be in. Sometimes he comes laughing and bearing gifts. He swings his son into the air and gives him bear hugs of affection. Other times he storms in the house in a foul, violent mood. Now what is the effect of the father's behavior on the son? We know the son is fearful of him because he has suffered at his father's hands. Yet, he still hopes every night that this will be one of the good times, and he is relieved and happy when he is right. As objectionable as the wide mood swings are, they are made much more damaging because they are unpredictable. The son never knows the disposition his father will be in when he enters the door; he has no way of knowing; and the anxiety and suspense he feels eats away at him. He can never truly relax or feel peace. He remains guarded and on edge, hoping but cringing at the same time.

The son is caught in an approach/avoidance conflict. He wants his father in his life and desires the relationship to be a positive, loving one. However, if the son achieves his goal of having his father be a part of his world, it also means he must endure unwanted, negative interchanges as well. This conflict becomes a source of great stress. If the situation were more predictable it would be clear to the son whether he should approach or avoid his father. Consider the difference if the son knows his father will always come home in a bad mood. That is, indeed, unpleasant, but at least he knows what to expect and can be prepared in any way he can devise. He may know he needs to hide, or to be silent, or to do something that will please his father. He retains some measure of control. He is no longer conflicted; he understands it is all about avoidance.

Fortunately, sad examples such as the one illustrated, though they do exist in real life, are not common. I used such a graphic instance only because parents so often fail to realize the importance of predictability in fostering feelings of security in their children. How, then, do we see the need for predictability play out in ordinary lives? In essence, we want our children to trust us; to know we will try to do the right thing. Anything short of that is far, far from the ideal. Ideally, they can predict we will respond to their needs with compassion and wisdom.

From the time babies are born they seek for pattern to explain the world; they begin to recognize the actions and the sounds which repeat themselves over and over again. The incoming stimuli become predictable. Babies come to know what sequences they should pay attention to and which ones they can safely ignore. This brings order to their world. Abrupt or unexpected changes to their accustomed schedules will be unsettling for them. Therefore, the watchwords for babies are slow and gentle when we are altering the agenda or context of the world with which they have become familiar.

For example, a mother may be weaning an infant from the breast to the cup. As most mothers discern, this must be done in steps and over time. It is the same with the other markers of change such as toilet training or sleeping in a "big girl's" bed. Bringing home a new baby requires significant pre-birth preparations because this certainly is not part of the predictable world of the toddler. It is up to the parents to make the idea of a new addition to the family familiar and natural. Maintaining as much of the old routine as possible after the new baby arrives home will help the toddler feel more settled and secure. When arriving home from the hospital after delivery I handed the new baby to my husband to carry into the house, so that my arms would be free to lovingly greet that little person who had so recently been displaced as the "youngest" and who now played a new role in the family dynamic.

The need to know what to expect continues throughout the years of growing and developing. It is freeing to know the rules of the household. Knowing the expectations of the parents makes it easier for the child to obey. (We will revisit this idea when we talk about training and obedience.) Predictability, in the context we are discussing here, refers more to how consistently a child can predict the actions and reactions of his parents. Will they maintain the values they espouse in all situations? Or will parents' actions depend on how they feel at the moment—angry, irritated, concerned, or even indifferent?

Mothers, by virtue of being more available, are frequently the ones who respond to the predicaments, crises, questions, and requests of their children. It is desirable that we respond predictably, in ways that harmonize with the principles of good mothering. For example, we need to exercise care in interpreting a problem in order to keep it from growing into something larger than it was in the first place. This means taking care not to overreact. Remaining calm and deliberate while considering an issue keeps it from taking on a life of its own and tones down the rhetoric. The trite but true counsel to abstain from making molehills into mountains is pertinent here. If the occasional "mountain" presents itself, even it does not need to become a Mount Everest. Staying focused, limiting the discussion to the known facts of the situation, and keeping an objective perspective helps. Many times when one of the children would adamantly accuse another person of unkind motivations by saying, "he (she) thinks . . . ," I would remind them that there is no way of getting inside another person's head to make such a judgment about motive. The dialogue should be reality-based and remain a reasoned one.

It may seem evident that if a mother wants to respond appropriately to the concerns of her children she needs to be a good listener; yet because of our great desire to keep our children from making mistakes it is tempting to jump in quickly to admonish or correct. That is an effective way of either escalating the emotions surrounding the issue or bringing the conversation to an end. If we want to remain part of the discourse, and it is vital that we do so, we must restrain these inclinations and exercise patience. When it comes to predictability one of the best expectations our children can have of us is that we will listen. Regardless of the substance, seriousness, or urgency of their plea, we will listen—calmly, completely, and with focus.

At times, a listening ear is all a child needs. Speaking aloud the pros and cons of a situation requires the speaker to categorize and analyze his or her thoughts in order to have the statements make sense to the listener. The resulting clarification may be all that a son or daughter needs, and we serve only as a willing listening post. Other times, however, advice and direction may be required. It may come in the form of teaching a new precept, applying an old truth to a new situation, giving a fresh perspective on the issue, or just reminding them of something they already know. The tricky part is to know how much to say. If all the child wants is a confirmatory nudge in the right direction, and we overwhelm with a long treatise on the subject, he or she may think twice before coming to us the next time. Recently, one of my single children, a university student, was worrying aloud about keeping up in classes because so many other activities were interfering. I could see what the problem was, but I knew he could see it as well. I just told him that I was feeling my motherly lecture on prioritizing responsibilities welling up inside me and asked him if he wanted to hear it. He just laughed and assured me he already knew what he should do to correct the situation.

Perhaps the most important expectation our children can have of us as parents, or specifically as mothers, is that we will try to live our convictions. It is a blessed home when the children in that home can rely on their parents to give them sound advice, and can further assume their parents will live the principles they espouse to the best of their ability. Though our children well know that we are not perfect and make many mistakes, they can feel the assurance that comes when they know our intentions are noble. For example, though we as parents often fell short in many ways, our children could predict that, barring illness or other unusual circumstances, we would all be in church on Sunday because of our heartfelt belief in its value. We did not discuss whether we wanted to go or not; it was not part of the conversation. Our children may at some time during their lives examine how they feel about church attendance, but they have the consistency of our example as a guide. And such was the case in regard to many issues.

Now may I draw an important distinction and give a qualifier to what I have said about predictability. Though it is an essential underpinning to a well-ordered family and to feelings of security, it should not become so controlling as to deaden the atmosphere in the home. It is important to distinguish between those things that should always remain the same (such as the virtues just mentioned above) and the day-to-day activities and events that make up the rhythm of our lives. While it is advisable to calendar events and follow daily schedules so all family members can be where they need to be and accomplish what they need to accomplish, there should be flexibility as well. It is nice, on occasion, to interrupt the humdrum and do something spontaneous. There is usually nothing unalterable about lists or agendas. Schedules are helpful in directing our energies so that we are efficient and effective, but they are only tools. Taking advantage of an unexpected opportunity, or feeling an impression to alter the plans for the day, may be exactly right.

For mothers who are living in close proximity to their children on a daily basis this is especially meaningful. I believe mothers develop a sense for when boredom or agitation cannot be countered by the usual means, and a change of scenery or mood is in order. When mothers leave the tub-scrubbing to get down on the floor and build a fort, or get up from the sewing machine to take part in a merry dance, that's great. It is part of our reality that the chores need to get done, but sometimes the dishes and laundry can wait. I remember on a whim taking the children for a leisurely stroll to pick flowers to cheer up an apartment that had become too small and confining.

Since the balance between predictable order and spontaneity is a delicate one, how do we recognize the best option? Once again, I recommend that we make our choice by determining the best thing for the child in that moment. It is certainly good for children to live in a clean and orderly home and to eat nourishing and well-prepared food—and achieving those goals takes time and effort—but it is also good for them to feel enlivened, to reach out, and to expand their horizons. What does the moment require? Fortunately, a spontaneous departure from the norm is usually a positive one, and mothers may "schedule" free time for just that purpose. Filling the day from dawn to dusk with projects, though worthy, may limit creative possibilities.

As children get older, it may be even more important to be flexible with schedules and demands. The unexpected comes more frequently to the teenager, and finding the right balance between scheduled responsibilities and spontaneous possibilities can be difficult. If we mothers make certain the values of the family and the everyday rhythms of home life remain a stable backdrop to their busyness, adolescents will continue to experience feelings of security. Teenagers generally encounter emotional highs and lows, new to them, as they transition between childhood and adulthood; and it is vital that the home remain a steadying force in their lives. We will speak more about this subject later on when we consider the topic of guidance, but as a general observation, I believe routine, predetermined activities should be the rule, and unscheduled changes should be the exception.

As we try to emulate the parenting of our Heavenly Father it serves us well to remember that He is predictable. We have the certainty of knowing that the Lord is neither random nor erratic with His children. We know what we may expect from Him as we read, "For behold, I am God; and I am a God of miracles; and I will show unto the world that I am *the same yesterday, today and forever*; and I work not among the children of men save it be according to their faith" (2 Nephi 27:23, emphasis added). We come closer to achieving the divine ideal when our children know what to expect from us, particularly regarding areas of moral certitude. Our children should be able to rely on us to keep their world, as near as we can, sane, secure, and predictable.

Accessibility

As children become increasingly self-aware they also come to realize their limitations. They know they are not as strong, as knowledgeable, as experienced, or as self-disciplined as the adults in their lives. Regardless of any attempt to appear otherwise, they keenly feel these inadequacies and need the continual (if often unspoken) assurance that one or more trusted, responsible adults will be available to help them handle life.

Obviously, the more dependent a child, the more important accessibility becomes. A newborn baby can only fuss and cry whenever she is uncomfortable. Whether this new little person learns to trust and feel secure in the world depends on how quickly and how well her needs are met. The time lag between the cry of distress and the response to the need should be as short as possible for an infant. At such a tender age the only thing babies come to understand is either that a loving person will warmly respond to their cries, or that they will be ignored. It is frightening for small children to discover that no matter how much they cry and scream for help it will do no good. This is a truism at any age when we think about it. What if we, in this very moment, urgently needed something and no one would respond? Suppose, no matter what we did, our pleas were ignored? That is scary, and such a scenario may produce feelings of insecurity regardless of our age.

Some babies have times when they suffer from colic and cannot be comforted. Occasionally (more than occasionally in the experience of some mothers), the crying is so unremitting that it becomes physically impossible for the mother to respond to the baby without getting some much needed rest herself. I recall one of my infants going through a time such as this when I walked the floor, bounced on the side of the bed, and tried everything I could think of to soothe the pain—but to no avail. Finally, when the nights grew too long and my strength began to give out, I would set the timer for ten minutes and lay the baby in his bed while I rested. In ten minutes I would pick him up again and try to give whatever comfort I could for the next forty minutes, and then repeat the ten-minute rest. Fortunately, this colicky period did not last long. One of my daughters exemplified true devotion as she experienced such challenges with all her babies, over longer periods of time, and welcomed any help she could get from family and friends. The bottom line here is that we do all we can to smooth the way for these little spirits. We accept whatever aid is offered to help us meet their need, and we trust in our Heavenly Father to make up the difference for whatever we are unable to handle on our own.

However, we might ask: If we give in to every demand would not that increase the likelihood of spoiling the child? Would it not be better to put into place some limitations on children and teach them what behaviors will be tolerated? The answer to that is both yes and no. Here it depends almost entirely on the age of the child. You cannot spoil young babies. They only cry when something is not right in their narrow world. They are often hungry or tired, wet or cramped, too hot or too cold, feeling gassy or constipated. Babies sometimes fuss when nothing seems to be wrong, and miraculously feel better when they are picked up. Are they spoiled? No, their needs are just broader in scope than the parents realized. We often expect that infants should be happy if they are clean, well-fed, and rested—and we usually look to meeting these physical needs first. But what about needs that go beyond the physical? What about the emotional, intellectual, and social ones? What if a baby is crying for attention, for companionship, for interaction, or for stimulation?

I had babies who were much easier to keep happy if their stimulation needs were met. I used to take them in their infant carrier with me as I worked in a room. I would rotate the little seat around every time they began to fuss in order to provide them a fresh view. In the kitchen, where so much work had to be done, I would open cupboard doors so the scene before them was more complex and interesting. Even then, I often had to leave the work before it was finished in order to pick them up for a little one-on-one time, and then relocate our activity to another room with different surroundings.

When a mother is in close proximity to a baby throughout the day she can better assess what level of stimulation is needed in that moment. For example, if I knew a fussy baby had been swaddled all day I might remove his clothing for a rub down and some freedom of movement. Other times may pose the opposite problem, where the infant had been over-stimulated or handled too much, in which case being wrapped securely again may be reassuring and settling for this small son or daughter. Being able to make a good assessment of a baby's needs requires being attuned to subtle shifts in mood and can only be accomplished when we as mothers are attentive and available.

Babies in good health learn something every day. Their brains are growing at an amazing rate as sensory input comes in and connections are made and then strengthened with each new input. At first they learn to recognize the warm, soothing voice that responds to their cries, and they come to expect gentle ministrations when a certain face appears on the scene. As they develop they begin to tell people apart and learn where they, themselves, end and someone else begins. They grow interested in their surroundings: the colors, movement, sounds, smells, and textures in their world. They want to be where the action is, to be included, to be safely in someone's arms as they explore their expanding world. Providing that patterned world in which the ministrations they have grown to expect are realized is a key component of good mothering.

Some theorists in psychology and other related fields have suggested that if a caretaker refuses to respond to a baby's cries, the infant can be trained to behave in more accommodating ways. This is true. It is possible to put the parents' needs first and shape a child's behaviors to suit the convenience or inclinations of the mother and father. For example, a baby can be trained not to cry for food or comfort during the night. If a baby's cries are ignored long enough he will cease to cry. It is well known that if the unwanted behavior is not rewarded it will eventually die out. The problem here is that something else may die as well: a feeling of trust and security, of knowing that someone is watching over him. Withdrawing rather than remaining accessible may well come at a steep price.

As children grow, they will learn there are other needs in the world besides their own; they will gradually develop some patience. Newborns know nothing of any other world besides the narrow one related to their sense of well-being, but babies three or four months old will know that their cries have been heard when they hear their mother's voice assuring them that she is coming and will be there momentarily. Merely speaking to the infant will substitute for action—for a short while. The infant knows Mother is close by and that she has heard him. Older infants can be distracted longer and the fulfillment of their needs can be delayed if necessary. In the give-and-take that is part of the natural rhythm of family life, a child learns patience. He comes to know that because gratification is delayed—it doesn't mean that it is not coming. By the time children are toddlers, they can be reasoned with in an elementary fashion and can understand that they must wait while Mommy finishes changing baby Nancy's diaper, or fills the washing machine.

As children begin to distinguish between their own and others' needs, it is time for parents to exercise caution in meeting every demand, even if they are able to do so. At this point, children can be spoiled if they are permitted to consider only their own wants. It remains imperative to maintain accessibility, to be certain the child understands she is safe, that Mom is in charge, and any genuine, urgent need the child has will be acted upon immediately—but all other needs and wants will be considered relative to the needs of others. Children can, over time, be trained to tell the difference between wants and needs, and will come to better understand why some needs are not as great as others. One of the tasks of mothering is to teach a child to be unselfish and attentive to the needs of other people.

At times parents may feel that if they are too accessible they will undermine a child's ability to eventually become a self-sufficient individual. If one were to survey parents about the ultimate goals they have for their children, it is likely that near the top of the list would be the desire to have their children grow into confident, independent adults. Sometimes the word "independent" can confuse a caring mother. How do we help a child become independent if we are always available?

We cannot let the word "independent" fool us. It is a noble goal to help children become self-reliant, but security cannot be diluted. In fact, security is a prerequisite to becoming independent. It has been shown that babies and children who have felt secure while growing up are more likely to be independent when they are grown. Withdrawing accessibility to Mother, or pushing a child away prematurely in the mistaken notion that the child needs to "grow up" and stop being a baby, does not promote genuine independence in that child. It will only alarm him more. If a baby wants to snuggle, then we snuggle. If a one-year-old wants to always be near us, we let her. If a preschooler wants to keep us in sight, that is fine.

But, here is a big caution: This is not about us. We need to do whatever is right for the child. When a secure child is ready to venture we permit it. We should not hover or over protect. We are present and available for hugs and reassurances, but we do not smother. A toddler may tentatively explore a new environment and then look around for Mom just to be sure she is still there. A smile and a nod may be all that is necessary. Perhaps the child lurches back to Mom's lap for a few moments of contact or a quick hug and then moves away once more, content that all is well. Being available does not mean doing everything for a child. We are their security not their servant. If a child is to be well trained, which we will address later, a mother should give no more than careful coaching when the child has the ability to do something for himself.

If life gets a little bumpy for an older child and she needs to retreat temporarily, that is okay. We need to be there for her, and she will usually move on when security is reestablished. An example that illustrates this concept comes to mind. One of our daughters was about five years old when our family moved across the country into married student housing so that my husband could pursue an advanced degree. Though she had seemed quite secure and unafraid up to this point, she began to have nightmares and would wake up crying and frightened. When she came into our bedroom for reassurance, I would pull her into bed with us until she felt calm. As this problem continued and I was now alert to it, I would listen for her, and when she woke up frightened I would go to her bed to be with her and we would talk about what worried her. As she confided that the mice in her dreams had long tails which could wrap around her neck and choke her, I never laughed at her fears or trivialized them.

Rather, we would examine the room as I reassured her that all was safe, and we would have a prayer together. I then gave her options. She could come into bed with us if she felt like she needed to; she could stay in her bed with a light on; or she could stay in her bed with just the hall light on and her door ajar. The degree of accessibility was under her control. I knew she did not really want to sleep with me and her father for the rest of her life and that she would be happy to sleep in the room with her sisters, and with the door closed, when she was ready. It did not take long for her to feel more secure in our new home, and for the problem to dissipate and not return. Had I said that she should not be such a "scaredy cat," that she was too big now to sleep with Mom and Dad, or that she would just have to get over it, her sense of security would have suffered.

When it is best for a child to have some added stimulation in his life beyond what he is receiving at home, this can be achieved without threatening his sense of security. Though I had not chosen to use preschools for my children, when my lastborn was four years old he was feeling at loose ends because his brothers and sisters were at school all day. It was new for him to have no one around during the day to play with, so I enrolled him in a small neighborhood preschool for a few hours twice a week. He enjoyed the songs and stories with his little friends. The key to making this work was that he never *had* to go. It was always his choice. Making the separation from Mom optional gave him a feeling of control over the situation, preserved his sense of security, and still allowed him a little adventure.

Shy or fearful children may need extra encouragement. It may require resourcefulness and ingenuity to help such children expand beyond the familiar and comfortable life they know. As I write this, I have a small grandson who is unsure whether kindergarten ought to be any part of his life. His parents are helping him acclimate to the idea of school by talking about it, touring it, and preparing his clothes and supplies. I have recommended that they keep all of this low-key and non-threatening. It is possible that Mom can be a teacher's assistant for a while until her little student gets acquainted and feels at ease in his class; or perhaps attending school can be postponed for a year to allow for developmental maturity to make a difference. Most important, forcing him, kicking and screaming, away from his secure place is not the answer.

As children move into the school years and become involved in the world of teachers, friends, sports, and free time, they spend more and more time away from Mom; their need for accessibility changes but does not disappear. She is no longer within arm's length of the child, but she is not far away either. The mother is removed enough to allow her child to stretch and grow, but near enough to support and guide. Ideally, she should be no more than a phone call away at this point. Being able to respond promptly or without much delay to a call from the school or other place away from home is important through these years. Accidents, illness, social challenges, and the unexpected are a part of life and will come to the school-age child as well. For children it is important for them to know that help and comfort will be quick in coming should they require it.

Such calls for assistance were a common occurrence for me through the years, and I felt grateful I could respond. On one occasion, two of our elementary-age sons were riding double on a bike down the hill near our home, returning to school after the lunch hour, when one of the boys caught his toe in the spokes of the rear wheel and sent them flying face-first into the asphalt on the pavement. One of their friends sprinted up the hill to our house to get me. How glad I was that I was near, that I could immediately take control of the situation, reassure them, and transport two very pitiful-looking little boys to the doctor so their injuries could be assessed and the road rash treated and cleaned out of their faces.

Such timely responses to emergencies clearly promote feelings of security in children, but being on hand to help with day-to-day challenges is important as well. All people have the need to talk over their concerns, and as a child grows into a teen, those concerns become weightier. As mothers we have an opportunity to serve as a sounding board, an empathizer, a trusted counselor, or even just an attentive audience. One of my fondest memories of the children as they came home from school was hearing the jokes they had heard that day or the funny things that happened at school. Other times they were tired, discouraged, or concerned about something that had happened during the day. The experiences adolescents encounter away from home can be mundane, encouraging, tiring, boring, fulfilling, frustrating, depressing, exciting—you get the picture. There are many ups and downs and every emotion is fair game. There are the successes of being elected class secretary, or being asked to the prom; there are the failures of striking out in the season baseball finals, or having your backpack break, spilling everything in the hall at school. And countless other events, large and small.

What is an adolescent to do with all these emotions? Being unable to express negative emotions and bottling them up inside can lead to depression or aggression; expressing them to the wrong people may lead to humiliation, inaccurate feedback, poor advice, or feelings of regret. Young people need to have someone interested in them and what is happening to them. If they do not have parents or other available and committed adults, they may turn to misguided friends, cliques, or gangs in order to be heard and to belong. Even if children are fortunate enough to have good friends in whom they can confide and share concerns, there are some things for which they need mature guidance from a trusted source, someone who they know has their welfare uppermost in mind. We, as mothers, need to arrange our lives so that we are available when our children need our counsel, just as we try to be when they need our assistance in day-to-day practical matters. In order to be there for a child in the ways we have discussed, we need to *be there*.

Oftentimes, hearing or addressing the concerns of a young person can be postponed with no harm done. If a problem is of some significance, choosing a time and place to discuss it later may be appropriate. Other times the emotion is in the moment and, whether happy or sad, needs to be expressed at the time it is felt. If we are not available when our children feel they need to share, they may go elsewhere; the moment of sharing will pass and we will have missed out on some very important information that could have helped us understand and better meet the needs of that child—had we known it. Some missed opportunities occur, of course, in every family. We mothers have other demands and distractions. We need to transport everyone where they need to go after school, whether it is a ball game, a music lesson, or an after-school job. A trip to an orthodontist appointment may provide a mother one-on-one time with a child—but perhaps not with the child who is in need of attention at that time.

Even if we are not needed elsewhere, we may be present but not listening. When I canned tomatoes for hours while the children were in school and needed help cleaning up the kitchen, or I had tended sick children all day and needed to have the clean laundry put away, I looked forward to the children coming home. I needed their help; I was not anxious to converse at length. It was more difficult at those times to get beyond my own concerns, and I am sure I was less attentive when I was worried about something else. Though I usually managed to have the laundry done, the house put in order, and dinner preparations underway before the children came in from school, some days I was less organized. Children understand such things, but their overall perception should be that you care about them and want to hear what they are thinking, doing, and feeling. If a child (or a husband, for that matter) ever says, "I need to tell you something," we should be attentive. Ensuring such natural proximity may seem easy, but oftentimes it takes concerted effort to arrange the day so that we are around when the children are home.

As I think about timing and accessibility, I recall the times when one or more of the children and I would stay up late talking. Why at such an hour? Simply, that was the time when they needed to talk. My four oldest children were girls, very close in age, and when they began dating, attending school and church functions at night, and working part-time, one would, at times, come home with something on her mind. Since I would be awake waiting for her, the five of us would talk, often about some very important topics. Other times, some of the children and I would just get talking and the discussion was important enough to continue past the normal bedtime.

At the time, my husband was not in favor of these extended conversations as he believed firmly in having a schedule (and even in following it!). Getting proper amounts of sleep and being able to get up early and refreshed were important to me as well, and I limited the times we stayed up later than normal, but today it would be difficult for me to put a value on what we gained in those impromptu conversations. The subjects we discussed were not trivial, as those could wait for more suitable hours. During these quiet, undisturbed times we discussed some of the most important lessons we need to learn in life, and I believe it benefited the children to speak their concerns aloud, to question, to listen, to recognize truth, and to learn to think for themselves. My husband has since recognized that these unscheduled interchanges were of considerable worth, not only because I chose to be available when the timing was right, but for the connectedness it brought to the family.

There was a period when I became concerned that the accessibility I valued so much might be compromised because of the large size of our family. I was an undergraduate in psychology at the time and had encountered studies which pointed toward some potentially negative outcomes for children when they were members of a large family. Their concern was that if a mother had many children she could not spread herself thin enough to provide all the stimulation and attention each child needed for healthy development. As I gave this subject careful consideration and reflected on our own household, I came to a few conclusions of my own.

It is true that one-on-one time with any particular child decreases as the number of children in the family increases, but that appears not to be an issue when the critical elements of a child's environment are in place. Being in a household with others is actually very invigorating and stimulating. Something interesting is going on all the time. No mother could begin to duplicate the numerous pursuits and hobbies taking place in a busy home. And though the children had their disagreements and irritations, they liked one another and enjoyed having each other in their lives as they worked and played. Sometimes at night when I would do a bed check I would see one of the little ones curled up in bed with an older brother or sister. That is wonderful! Any love, attention, training or enriching interaction is appreciated—no matter where it comes from— and that very feature is one of the strengths of a large family.

Notwithstanding the contributions of supportive siblings, a mother's accessibility remains the critical element. There will be a lot going on in such a home, but ideally a mother should remain in close proximity so that she may direct, answer questions, help solve problems, have timely conversations, and express love. When a small child gets tired no one but Mom will do. She should be available to pull a child onto her lap for comforting or quiet time. She should be there when one-on-one time is needed with any of her children. The other children in the family cannot replace or substitute for the primary caretaker; indeed we mothers should avoid burdening older children with inappropriately heavy caretaking responsibilities. Mothers who leave the home because older children are around to take her place are moving away from the ideal. Mother's accessibility helps to ensure that a large family, or any family, will thrive.

Working Mothers

The accessibility issue may be one of particular concern if you are a working mother. Because a significant percentage of mothers work outside the home this is an area of considerable consequence and merits particular attention within the general topic of accessibility. Over many years, much discussion has taken place pertaining to the advisability of a mother working away from home, especially when the children are young. I have a few thoughts I would like us to consider as we ponder this question, but I need to preface those remarks with a fervently held conviction: the decision of whether or not to work is a personal one. It is not for others looking on to judge. Ultimately, only the parents, in prayerful consideration of Gospel teachings, can make such an important decision.

Traditionally, mothers have been the bearers and nurturers of the new generation. As mothers began entering the workforce in increasing numbers there was much debate as to how such a societal shift would affect children. We were essentially undertaking a massive sociological experiment, and strongly-held views developed on both sides of the debate. At-home mothers defended their position that they were indispensable to the upbringing of their children. Working mothers felt conflicted and guilty about their absence since they loved their children as much as at-home mothers did, yet felt they were making an important contribution elsewhere or that they had to work to help support their families.

The question began to be couched in terms of quantity versus quality. It was suggested that if a mother chose to stay at home the quality of her caregiving would suffer. She was sometimes portrayed as a haggard, depressed, discontented person, answering the door in a rumpled sweat suit, with her children running around unsupervised. She was there, putting in the time, but the benefits to the children were questionable. On the other hand, though a working mother was portrayed as busy and sometimes harried, the career woman was frequently portrayed as being fulfilled by virtue of being valued for her work outside the home, and she was therefore in a better frame of mind to give quality care to her children when she arrived home.

In order to make sense of the questions surrounding the working mother I think we need to recall that the primary principle of mothering is to do what is best for the child. Each mother needs to discover what is optimal for her family and do that. In order to make such a decision, however, it helps to know what the ideal would be if we lived in a perfect world. With such a vision we are better able to approximate the ideal. Though none of us will ever be a perfect mother in this world, if we can more clearly picture the ideal we can come closer to approaching that goal. It is important to remember, therefore, that we are not speaking here of choosing between quantity and quality. In a perfect world we would not have to choose between the two. This is not an "either/or" question. Elder M. Russell Ballard confirmed this understanding:

"Taking care of small, dependent, and demanding children is never ending and often nerve-racking. Mothers must not fall into the trap of believing that 'quality' time can replace 'quantity' time. Quality is a direct function of quantity—and mothers, to nurture their children properly, must provide both. To do so requires constant vigilance and a constant juggling of competing demands."[1] As we continually measure our efforts against the perfect model we will try to provide both quantity and quality, because ideally children should have both.

While in graduate school I researched the effects of daycare on infants and young children—looking in-depth at every source I could find on the subject. Though most studies determined that the majority of children exposed to day care would grow up to be happy, well-adjusted human beings, some red flags were raised. Variables such as the age of the child when first going into day care, the length of time spent in day care per day (and over time), the quality of the facility, and other factors, played into the resulting effects—with some of those effects being statistically negative.

As previously mentioned, I felt my last child benefited from spending a few hours in preschool each week. There is a caution with preschools, day care facilities, and other child placements, however. Even if the child attends willingly and enjoys the experience, the time spent in that setting should be limited if at all possible. Developmental studies have shown that the first five years of a child's life are critical in the forming of values and the way she views the world. Because it is such a formative period of life it is vital to use that time well—giving the child a solid, careful, secure foundation on which to build a life and develop a healthy personality. Such foundational work can best be directed when a child is under the guidance of wise, caring parents.

Some research has found that children who spend long hours in preschools or day care tend to become more peer-oriented, or in other words they tend to cue off their friends. In contrast, those who spend those formative hours at home tend to look to their parents. This early "cueing" tendency may become part of their personalities, and as teenagers they may continue to take their cues from their friends, making the influence of their peer group more powerful than it otherwise would have been. Those children who look to their parents for guidance are more inclined as teenagers to continue to be guided and influenced by them. During the angst of adolescence it is obvious that a teenager, who will still listen to the mature voices of his parents rather than the sometimes impetuous and unwise voices of his contemporaries, will likely have a safer passage through the challenges associated with this stage of life.

President James E. Faust affirmed this research finding: "Generally, those children who make the decision and have the resolve to abstain from drugs, alcohol, and illicit sex are those who have adopted and internalized the strong values of their homes as lived by their parents. In times of difficult decisions they are most likely to follow the teachings of their parents rather than the example of their peers or the sophistries of the media, which glamorize alcohol consumption, illicit sex, infidelity, dishonesty, and other vices."[2]

Mothers are critical to this undertaking as their influence is early and enduring. The Prophet Brigham Young said: "The duty of the mother is to watch over her children and give them their early education, for impressions received in infancy are lasting."[3]

Since it may be necessary to use more day care than is ideal it helps to approach that ideal by choosing such alternative care carefully. Smaller clusters of children are generally easier to monitor and manage than are larger groups. Caretakers should be chosen who reflect the values of the parents and who will make the effort to lead and supervise interactions among the children. How children are allowed to treat one another and how their attitudes toward authority are shaped is especially important. It is of interest to note that one of the reasons some parents give for teaching their children at home is their desire to avoid the increasing disrespect for parents, teachers, and other authority figures, often found among children.

Without detailing all the concerns uncovered in investigations of alternative child care we can ask ourselves some important and revealing questions: Can anyone else love this child of mine as much or as well as I do? Do the caretakers worry about the welfare of my child more than they do about their own welfare—just as I do? Will they set aside other distractions and take the time to hold and cuddle my baby as I would? Do they even have the time to do so with so many to care for? Are they always available and will they respond quickly to signs of distress? Do they know my child and his needs as well as I do? Will they keep her stimulated and engaged, and will they use appropriate discipline kindly?

Since we cannot in fairness expect a paid caretaker to be as invested and loving as the mother, these may seem like unfair questions to ask.

Actually, they serve to reveal how far we are moving away from the idyllic model we seek to emulate when we consider a substitute for Mother.

However, when a mother has no choice but to obtain child care, it is necessary to ask a different question: how far from the ideal can we safely stray? There are many loving and caring caretakers. If a mother must find a substitute for herself, finding a caretaker who mirrors her values and loving attention is important—as is retaining the same caretaker over time since change often introduces insecurity. If we cannot live the ideal, we should approximate the ideal as nearly as possible.

Some studies have shown that children who are reared by caregivers other than their mothers do well as long as the principles spoken of in this book are in force. For example, the father may play a larger caregiving role in the home than the mother for a period of time (or even for years if he is a single father). In some circumstances it is not uncommon for grandparents to rear their grandchildren in their own homes. Sometimes, multigenerational families made up of parents, grandparents, or other relatives such as uncles, aunts, and cousins, live together with the children. Such arrangements may provide multiple caregivers for a child. Often this can be a loving and lively environment for children and they thrive; other times some of the principles so important to a child's upbringing are largely absent and the child suffers.

We may wonder why there is a continued emphasis on keeping Mother as the primary nurturer if other combinations of caring individuals will suffice. President Gordon B. Hinckley has expressed the answer succinctly: "I remind mothers everywhere of the sanctity of your calling. No other can adequately take your place."[4] Beyond any pronouncements by experts or research studies in the field, the mother is to nurture children because it is the pattern given to us by the Lord.

In The Family, a Proclamation to the World,[5] we are offered an inspired guide for family happiness. From it we are to understand that mothers and fathers have divinely appointed responsibilities that should be faithfully performed to the best of their abilities as conditions permit. In circumstances where one or the other of them needs help with their obligations, the other partner provides whatever assistance is necessary and appropriate. In family life we see this happening at every level. When we had a new baby in the home my husband would see to the needs of the toddler who awoke at night. I was up so frequently to nurse and care for the new little one that this helped me to get some rest in order to better handle the demands of the next day. At times when my husband was under considerable stress with work, school, and church responsibilities, I would relieve him as much as possible by taking care of his chores, such as seeing to the care of the car, taking out the garbage, and handling the correspondence and bookkeeping tasks. It was reassuring to know that even though we had our own stewardships, we were equal partners and we tried to always be there for one another. The children enjoyed it when their dad took care of them. Menus and routines altered enough to be interesting, and he kept them active and engaged.

Larger life events may change the dynamics of a family. As mentioned in the Proclamation, such things as disability or death may necessitate a departure from the ideal design. As we look at the lives of real women around us, we know there is sometimes a need for secure employment in order to care for the temporal needs of the family. A mother may lose a breadwinner to death or divorce or disability. In these circumstances the Lord is aware of the special blessings a mother needs when she is required to be out of the home. The extended family can frequently provide welcome assistance for a mother who needs to assume these additional responsibilities. When we consider the broad implications of doing what is right for the child we recognize that providing temporal sustenance is a fundamental requirement for any person, and sometimes that provider role falls to the mother.

Let us remind ourselves, however, that we are now making approximations of the ideal. I am sure a single father will tell you that life would be better for his family if a caring mother were a part of it. Working mothers would prefer to have the *option* of working, not the necessity. Grandparents, I am equally certain, would acknowledge that as much as they love and serve the little ones to whom they are devoting their lives, it would be better for the children to be in a family with a righteous mother and father living the divine design the Lord has outlined. When the adversities of life make living the perfect family lifestyle impossible, the Lord only asks us to do the best we can; He will make up the difference.

Mothers may choose to work for reasons other than providing adequate temporal provisioning. They may want to procure more for the family than one income can provide—perhaps a bigger house, an extra car, more clothes, or additional recreational opportunities. In the present day it often takes two incomes to provide for the standard of living we have come to expect. Parents want their children to feel that they are as good as their peers, and often think a child's self-esteem will suffer if they do not have as big a Christmas or as many toys or opportunities as their friends have. But is this true?

It is beyond the scope of this book to delve into all the issues surrounding the development of a solid self-esteem, but from both experience and study I know that self-esteem does not stem from what a person has, but from who a person is. It is about integrity and character, and about being able to contribute meaningfully. Children who learn skills that can be useful in helping others, feel good about themselves. (We will speak more about equipping children with self-affirming capabilities in a later chapter.) As children learn to focus on others rather than their own wants they lose the self-absorption that may eventually bring them so much grief. Too much attention to worldly acquisitions may detract from rather than aid in helping children to understand these truths.

For our purposes here we need to remind ourselves that the Proclamation tells us that by divine design it falls to the father, wherever possible, to provide the necessities of life. Elder Boyd K. Packer reminds us: "Some mothers must work out of the home. There is no other way. And in this they are justified and for this they should not be criticized. We cannot, however, because of their discomfort over their plight, abandon a position that has been taught by the prophets from the beginning of this dispensation."[6]

Some mothers contend they are not working for the extras, but for the basics. And that may well be true. Ours is largely a cash society now and it takes a lot of money to live. We want our children to be well-cared-for temporally, so what is the threshold we need to reach before we send mom into the workforce to bring home a second income? This, of course, can be determined only by the father and mother in consultation with the Lord. It is a private and personal matter, but may I make a few observations to think about as we contemplate this question?

Let us first consider standard of living. How high does it need to be? We all need to be comfortable, safe, and have some beauty in our lives; but can we achieve that on the father's income? If we moved to a less expensive neighborhood, moved into a smaller (maybe older) home, got by with one vehicle, gave up eating out, did without cable television, and either cut out or pared down many other aspects of our current lives, could we live within his income then? What if we went even further and gave up extended vacations, substituting camping trips near home, or did our own repairs, or made our own bread, could we do it then? It may be revealing if we were to calculate just how far we could stretch the father's income if that were all we had.

My husband and I have had to make such decisions. One afternoon, not long before we were married, Corrin and I stood under a large, shady tree talking about our future life together. We knew we wanted a large family and decided that twelve children sounded like a good number. That arbitrary figure, picked at random, meant only that we would have all we could. We believed in the timeless admonition of the Lord to multiply and replenish the earth. Brigham Young reminded the newly restored Church, "It is the duty of every righteous man and woman to prepare tabernacles of all the spirits they can."[7] We grew up with President David O. McKay as the Prophet and we believed in his admonition: "Members of the Church who are healthy and normal should not be guilty of restricting the number of children in the home, especially when such action is prompted by a desire for a good time, or for personal gain, or to have as much as the neighbors, or by a false impression that with only one or two children in a family they can be better educated. These are excuses that no one should harbor, for they are unjustified."[8] This instruction to have children has never been rescinded.

We understood, of course, that many things outside our control would play a part in the size of our family, and perhaps our only certainty was that we would welcome any spirits the Lord had in reserve for us. We were not so naïve as to assume it would be easy, and we knew my health as a mother would likely be the key consideration. We definitely knew it would be expensive. Yet we believed that if we had faith ways would be opened which would permit us to provide for any children the Lord gave us. Elder Boyd K. Packer recently gave this reassurance: "Do not be afraid to bring children into the world. We are under covenant to provide physical bodies so that spirits may enter mortality."[9] We believed it then, and we believe it still. We reared eleven children and there was always room at our table even though we lived on my husband's income as a public school teacher.

We also agreed that I should remain in the home where I could nurture the family—using the timeless principles of love and sacrifice. I admit we might have been a bit naïve on that score. We had no idea just how much sacrifice would be required. Corrin's salary would only stretch to meet all our needs if we did everything we could for ourselves. And so we did. When I describe how I ground wheat for bread-making, trimmed everyone's hair, transformed cow's milk into yogurt and cottage cheese, preserved many bushels of produce, and so on, I am reminded of the early, occasionally whimsical, stories of our grandparents where children had to walk to school . . . five miles . . . in the snow . . . going uphill both ways!

If you were to interview the children now I'm sure you would hear about the things they did not like about the need to be resourceful. I heard them complain they were the only ones in town who didn't have a VCR; they were hot and sweaty driving around in our car with its black interior and no air-conditioning; they had to duck so their friends would not see them when their dad took them to school in the old truck; they had to earn their own money for all the extras they needed; the younger ones tired of wearing their older brothers' or sisters' hand-me-downs; and so on. However, these complaints in the larger view and over time have not amounted to much. They served to educate the children in identifying the differences between wants and needs. We needed a car. We wanted one with air conditioning. We did not need to spend a lot of money on clothing; we only needed to look like we spent a lot of money.

In a world where ample money is considered necessary for the good life and for achieving happiness, we may view the smaller income resulting from a mother's decision to stay at home as an unacceptable sacrifice. We worry that our children will suffer hardship and difficulties. Perhaps they will miss out on some opportunities they might have had, or suffer from poor self-esteem. In this view, being accessible comes at too high a price for a mother, and so we trade accessibility for larger family earnings.

On the other hand, there is another view which makes a single income a blessing rather than a sacrifice. When limits are placed on the flow of money and material acquisitions, children's lives are blessed by the need to work, to cooperate, to conserve resources, and to consider the needs of the family as a whole. This will be true in any family, regardless of the abundance of its resources. For those families whose worldly wealth is more than just adequate it will take great wisdom and control to curb unwise expenditures and selfish expectations, but it can be done. Families who have to stretch their dollars will find it easier to recognize and apply appropriate limits, and single mothers usually will not suffer from a problem of over-abundance.

It may not be easy, and there were times when we were uncomfortably tight, but there were also a great many benefits, particularly for the children.

I found when we focused on needs instead of wants it was easier to count our blessings because our needs were always met. Contrariwise, wants are never satisfied no matter how bounteous earnings may be, and that can lead to dissatisfaction. We learned that hard work and ingenuity could often make up the difference between wants and needs, and that valuable insight triggered creative thinking. I tried to help the children see problems as challenges to be overcome, or even as adventures, and to stay positive by looking for the silver lining that was usually present in every difficulty. Such an approach to the problems in life helped to inoculate the children against learned helplessness.

Learned helplessness is an inability to overcome obstacles in life, even when there may be a way to do so. It is a sort of giving up or giving in to circumstances which are perceived as being insurmountable, albeit inaccurately. Children can be inoculated against this phenomenon when they are given opportunities to overcome difficulties. Learning to measure your challenges, think through your options, and muster your forces gives you control over what is happening to you. The confidence our children gain as they realize they can make a difference by applying themselves will stand them in good stead in the years to come, particularly if economic and other challenges grow more serious and courage and ingenuity are at a premium.

Even though it was an ongoing process to help our children see the comparative value of the many things in the world around them, it was absolutely imperative that Corrin and I understood the difference between wants and needs. Beyond the obvious basics of food, clothing, and shelter, we knew the children needed such things as good medical and dental care, orthodontia, music lessons, opportunities to learn and grow, and an exposure to great ideas. We worked hard to see that they received these benefits. Other things may or may not be possible. I felt disappointed at times when I could not afford to do some things for the children, such as taking them to the circus when it came to town, or going on long vacations to learn about the world. Yet, I knew those opportunities would come to them in time. In fact, I knew if we took great care in providing them security, love, spiritual preparedness, training, the seeds of curiosity, and a desire to understand the world, they could embrace that larger arena with confidence in due time.

I have good intentions in having working mothers consider feasible ways of making staying at home with their children a possibility. For many women the opportunity of being a full-time mother is the desire of their heart, and they would remain in the home if they could remove financial obstacles in order to do so. For some women this may be more possible than they have previously thought. Perhaps, on serious reflection, working mothers may see ways to make being at home possible, with the realization that needed changes might require significant sacrifices on their part and on the part of other family members.

Other working mothers may feel that being out of the home for some time every day makes them a better mother. Some women become depressed when they are cooped up too much or lack outside stimulation. These are genuine issues that must be considered and, once again, the decision needs to be based on what is best for the child. It may be better for the child to have a happy, content mother part time, than an unhappy mother full time. Only the mother can know how she can best carry out this stewardship. That is why someone from the outside cannot judge, and I do not judge. In fact, I am one of your cheerleaders. I know mothering is a one-of-a-kind experience that takes everything we can give it. Though it may be fulfilling and wonderful—even inspiring—it is also demanding, scary, and just plain hard work. I stand behind mothers every inch of the way and applaud all their efforts.

It is important to remember that the Lord will bless us as we do everything we can to be good mothers. We need to have a testimony of that truth and learn to trust Him to provide whatever we cannot. There were more times than I can count when I would put pencil to paper, trying to see how we were going to make our finances stretch over a certain time period or an unexpected event, and it just did not compute. Yet, it always worked out that we had enough. When we have desire and faith, the Lord will provide. I remember one time I was saving to get a little ahead, day-dreaming how I could use the extra money, when the vacuum went out. I had just enough to purchase a new one. A vacuum was hardly the item I had been envisioning, but I was grateful we had the money to buy one. The Lord knows our needs. Sometimes He uses others for this purpose and we find our extended families and friends unstinting in their support of our efforts.

A mother contemplating whether she can afford to come home from work should not forget to calculate in faith. President Boyd K. Packer gave this admonishment: "If Mother is working outside of the home, see if there are ways to change that, even a little. It may be very difficult to change at the present time. But analyze carefully and be prayerful (see D&C 9:8–9). Then expect to have inspiration, which is revelation (see D&C 8:2–3). Expect intervention from power from beyond the veil to help you move, in due time, to what is best for your family."[10] Our Father is the best partner we can have.

Whether we are working mothers or not, we must make personal decisions about how we will interface with the larger world. Though my life was wonderful and rewarding in the grand scheme of things, it was not grand in the day-to-day details of living; it often seemed thankless, filled with the same repetitive chores; and there were times when I would chafe under the unrelenting demands. I wondered how my talents were being used when I spent my time changing diapers and cooking hot cereal. How would I ever fulfill my desire for a higher education? Each time I prayed and pondered these questions I received the same answer: nothing in the world was more important than doing what was right for these children and centering their lives. The time and season for finishing my education was not yet. It was not until my eldest daughter graduated from a two-year college that I walked beside her in the graduation line and received my associate degree as well—and that was only the beginning. Years later, in the year 2000, I received my doctorate.

With patience and perseverance women can accomplish many good things in the course of their lives. Elder M. Russell Ballard quotes very wise counsel given by President James E. Faust: "A woman . . . may fit more than one career into the various seasons of life. She need not try to sing all of the verses of her song at the same time."[11] I believe it is possible to serve society and fulfill personal dreams; but the family should always be a mother's top priority.

Although I tried to apply the principle of accessibility as I raised my family, I did not do so perfectly; there was one occasion when I made a serious mistake in this regard and which I would like to describe, in the hopes that it may help other mothers to avoid a similar problem.

I spent some time at college before I married, and was able to fit in an occasional class afterward, but it was only after I had been an at-home mother for about twenty years that I began slowly working toward a college degree. I had been instructed to get this education in my patriarchal blessing, but had been impressed to wait until the family was complete and functioning securely before making the attempt. The children were older and supportive, and it seemed to work well. However, one year I found myself straining to maintain accessibility because of an error in judgment.

I had made an attempt to receive confirmation from the Lord regarding my plans for the educational year ahead, expecting, as I had always experienced before, an affirmative response. And though I did receive a feeling of peace and support as I contemplated a full year of school, I also received an unmistakable caution along with it—which came as a surprise. There came into my mind an admonition to be especially careful of the family, so that their welfare would not be compromised. Since this was a principle I had served and believed in over the years I assumed I would take care of that naturally; but part way into the school year I realized I had not been careful enough.

I found myself under considerable stress as I was finishing up my master's thesis, while at the same time taking a full load of doctoral course work. In addition (and I think this was my mistake), I agreed to teach a class of close to two hundred students the second semester. I thought at the time that it was a wonderful opportunity; I would enjoy it because I love teaching; it would look good on my resume; and most important, we could use the money. My husband was teaching full time and working home construction when he was not in school in order to provide for all our needs, which included providing the financial support for two of our children who were serving full-time missions at the same time. Even though he made no complaints about his heavy load and did not expect me to accept this offer of employment, I felt it would be helpful to our situation. I suppose it did help to bring in more money, but the financial help came at too steep a price.

I found myself not merely trying to get by one day at a time but one hour at a time. In addition to the heavy demands surrounding school and the considerable responsibilities and household chores of a big family, our missionaries and their concerns were never far from my mind. I was also concerned that two of our daughters had small children, some with colic, and could have used my help, and one daughter got married that year and bore more of the responsibility for planning her wedding than I thought she should have had to. I had taken on too much; I could not be everywhere and do everything I should; and my anxiety began to exact its toll.

I could see the family at home begin to strain as I had to shift more and more of my time and focus away from them. One of the younger children began to have stomachaches. I had the symptom checked out medically and was not surprised to discover these problems were likely due to psychological causes. The children were unaccustomed to a stressed, preoccupied mother.

When I could see the problem, I tried harder to maintain the consistency they had known and to provide a calmer and more relaxed atmosphere, but I knew my present circumstances were beyond anything I could do to repair in the short term. And I repented! I knew I had gone against counsel when I did not take seriously enough the caution I had received regarding the family. I pleaded with the Lord to forgive me, and to cushion the family from the pressures I had brought into our home until I could get things straightened out once more. Never again, I promised, would I put other considerations, even worthy ones, before my responsibilities as a mother. I felt such a love for my children, I did not think I could make a mistake such as this and I was humbled. The university class I taught turned out well; I really enjoyed the experience and the students. But that blessing should have been someone else's that year. We each have to do what is right for the child—and that had not been it.

There are many decisions we will need to make as mothers when we try to get the right balance in our lives. I learned to be patient in achieving goals, and to be willing to sacrifice for the good of the family. Looking back, I see that the things we had to go through are the very things that have brought us strength. The hard work, the togetherness, the knowledge that labor performed was truly needed and not just of token value, and many other lessons of life have been blessings to our children, now grown. My five married daughters and my two daughters-in-law have been blessed to be able to be at-home mothers. I hope those yet to be married will be as fortunate. It is not easy in a two-income society, but it remains the ideal and therefore worth working for.

I am comforted to know that for mothers who must secure outside employment, the Lord compensates, and their families are blessed accordingly. President Gordon B. Hinckley has addressed mothers who must provide financial means: "To you women who find it necessary to work when you would rather be at home, may I speak briefly? . . . I pray that the Lord will bless you with strength and great capacity, for you need both. You have the responsibilities of both breadwinner and homemaker. I know that it is difficult. I know that it is discouraging. I pray that the Lord will bless you with a special wisdom and the remarkable talent needed to provide your children with the time and companionship and love and with that special direction only a mother can give."[12]

For the rest of us, where choice and sacrifice are possible, the Lord will bless our families as we put our trust in Him and abide by His counsel. I still feel the same burning testimony I felt through all those years of struggle; our children are our greatest work. It is well worth our effort to remain as accessible to our children as our individual circumstances allow.

Both accessibility and predictability are an integral part of our children's security. We desire our children to flourish and to embrace life with joy and confidence.

Notes

1. M. Russell Ballard, "The Sacred Responsibilities of Parenthood," *Ensign*, Mar. 2006, 26–33.
2. James E. Faust, "A Thousand Threads of Love," *Ensign*, Oct. 2005, 2–7.
3. *Discourses of Brigham Young*, sel. John A. Widtsoe, (Salt Lake City: Deseret Book, 1946), 201.
4. Gordon B. Hinckley, "Bring up a Child in the Way He Should Go," *Ensign*, Nov. 1993, 60.
5. Family Proclamation, *Ensign*, Nov. 1995.
6. Boyd K. Packer, (talk to the All-Church Coordinating Council, Salt Lake City, UT, May 18, 1993).
7. *Discourses of Brigham Young*, sel. John A. Widtsoe, (Salt Lake City: Deseret Book, 1946), 197.
8. David O. McKay, "Our Greatest Obligation," *Liahona*, Oct. 1979, p. 12.
9. Boyd K. Packer, "Do Not Fear," *Ensign*, May 2004, 77–80.
10. Ibid.
11. Ballard, "The Sacred Responsibilities of Parenthood," 26-33
12. Gordon B. Hinckley, "Live Up to Your Inheritance," *Ensign*, Nov. 1983, 83

Chapter Four

Guidance and Training: Blueprints for Life

In our consideration of the principles of mothering imperative in every age and circumstance, we have addressed the needs for love and security. A third principle, just as necessary if our children are to grow up happy and fulfilled, is the need for guidance and training. Children do not grow up in a vacuum. Their world is filled with people and ideas. They must learn how to get along and work with others, and how to manage their time and resources. The demands of the world we live in are challenging and unrelenting. Among the greatest gifts we can give our children are the skills and attitudes they need to survive and thrive.

Every family offers a unique skill set in which the talents, interests, and choices of the parents will influence what is being taught or emphasized in that household. The diversity found among families is a plus in society, providing variety and excellence in many fields. However, certain precepts important in any living arrangement or in any family will be addressed here. I will continue to use examples from my own mothering experiences which reflect our own family's circumstances. These specifics will point to the timeless principles to which they apply.

Order

Because family members are "in training," an indispensable part of the home environment is order. It would be difficult to accomplish much if confusion and disorder reigned. To rummage under piles for something you need, or hunt through overflowing closets or packed drawers is time-consuming, inefficient, and frustrating. In addition to the clearly practical advantage of having a place for everything and everything in its place, orderliness brings with it mental clarity and peacefulness. We will certainly draw closer to, or approximate, the divine design if we can establish order. "Behold, mine house is a house of order, saith the Lord God, and not a house of confusion" (D&C 132:8).

Even though children are by nature hands-on (a nice term for messy), and they like to have plenty of props around them to use in their creative play, they respond positively to a well-ordered environment. I noticed as I completed cleaning and straightening a room in our home, the children would be drawn to that room. They would leave the mess they were busy creating somewhere else to enjoy the feelings of beauty and repose that orderliness brings. Everything was where it belonged. There was no jumble, nothing in disarray to jar the senses. Of course, the room would not remain that way because homes are where people live and grow, and the home should be used, not just admired. But there should be some level of organization. Clutter can overwhelm the hardiest of spirits—eventually.

Starting when they are very young, children can be taught to take care of their surroundings. Toddlers can put their balls back in the toy box, preschoolers can smooth their beds, and primary-age children can wash dishes and vacuum. Timing is important here because we do not want to discourage children by making demands beyond their capabilities to perform, but usually children can do more than we think they can. They love to be able to master tasks they see being done around them. I have a picture in our family album of one of our sons at the age of four, standing on a chair at the kitchen sink, enveloped in a big apron, washing the dishes. His hair is poking straight up, but he is contributing and he is happy.

Regrettably, by the time one has trained a child into being a good helper, mundane chores have lost their appeal, and a mother has to use her ingenuity to motivate children. I tried many ways of organizing work through the years, wheels, charts, and so forth, and most of them were effective for a short while, until the children grew bored. I admire families who develop a system that continues to work for them over time, but I never could. Once when a pregnancy kept me on the sofa or the bed some of the time, I had to find a way to inspire more help than I was currently receiving; so I turned us into a mini-army. I was the captain and the children were the soldiers. I labeled everything with military tags, such as "the mess hall" and "the latrine," and divided the chores into small sizes so the children had more opportunities to report to their captain with a smart salute and receive new orders. It worked, but only for a while.

One of the advantages of a large family is that everyone's help is needed. All our children baked bread from scratch, bottled fruit and tomatoes, put on healthy meals, took care of laundry tasks, mowed and weeded outside, and performed a multitude of other chores. Every skill children learn increases their usefulness and their confidence, and usefulness and confidence bring self-worth. Of note here, however, is that with so much activity going on, the need for order is essential. The ongoing bustle can degenerate into commotion unless direction and order are provided. This is particularly important when children are working together on a group project. Organization is necessary in group production so each person can understand and perform his task, and visualize how his role contributes to the group's common objectives.

When we bottled produce, for example, everyone had an assigned job. We had one or two "gofers" who brought in the bushels of produce, made sure we had clean bottles and lids, washed and scalded the fruit, and loaded and unloaded the filled bottles into the steamer. The rest of the team would sit at the table and peel, slice, pit, and so on, and occasionally run trays of fruit outside to the roof of the playhouse where the fruit could dry in the sun. This division of labor helped us to maintain the necessary order essential to efficient production.

In the interest of full disclosure, I just have to say here that this was hot, sticky, heavy work. No matter how efficiently we executed our work, the days were long and tiring. Sprinkled among the complaints about the heat, the peach juice running down our arms, and the peach fuzz itching us, we had great conversations as we worked; we laughed a lot, and I would try to think of every positive slant I could put on the labor at hand. I reminded the children how lucky they were to have a free spa treatment since the warm, steamy atmosphere would cleanse their pores and give them lovely complexions. (That is probably why they were laughing. This was in the same vein as the nice waistlines they got while weeding.)

Such well-ordered work yielded the results we were trying to achieve. The best part of the day seemed to be when the bottles were cooling on the counter, but it was really just the evidence of a good day. The important achievement was that we had hung in there. The children knew they had what it takes to get organized, to complete hard, physical, and sometimes unpleasant work over a long period of time, without giving up or giving in. They could sweat and itch, and grow weary and still stay the course. Such knowledge about themselves was as valuable as the rows of produce lining the shelves. One summer we processed (bottled, dried, and froze) twenty-one bushels of peaches alone. It has made a difference in my children's lives to learn the value of order, to know how to perform many tasks, to know they can contribute much-needed help, and to learn they are made of pretty tough stuff.

While order is necessary for group efficiency, it is also required in individual lives. As our children became more responsible for the care of their own rooms they learned the value of a well-kept personal space. Sometimes when they became overwhelmed with school and extracurricular activities they would neglect this aspect of their lives. Clean, well-pressed clothes were in short supply as clothing piles grew deeper on the bed. Homework and lessons had to be sorted from among stacks of books and papers. Hastily discarded makeup and jewelry were left lying around for younger brothers and sisters to investigate. It was not a pretty picture. Many times the appeals my husband and I made to the offenders to adhere to the rules of the household and to put their lives in order went unheeded, and it became necessary that they be required to see how unbalanced their lives had become. We were not hesitant to have them pare some of their activities if they were too burdened to live a balanced life. Especially when their disregard of this facet of their lives was impacting all other areas.

It was with a sense of relief that they crawled between clean sheets in a newly made bed after order had been reestablished in their rooms and in their lives. Their spirits were brighter, they felt more in control, efficiency was restored, and they were easier to live around. I wish I could say this cause and effect training only needed to be done once and the lesson was learned. Unfortunately, I cannot begin to count how many times this or a similar scenario played out over the years, but learning that particular lesson is so vital to the future productivity and fulfillment of an individual that it is worth the effort to teach, and they learned to recognize when their personal space was no longer functioning well for them and to take the necessary steps to gain control again.

Research on this topic has found that living in chaotic surroundings is one of the most difficult environments in which a child can be reared. It is not easy to sort our thoughts amid chaos. Establishing order in our environment is one way we learn to bring order to our minds—to be able to think clearly. Even authoritarian, too-strict parents are found to be preferable to lax, permissive parents who permit or encourage an anything goes, do-what-feels-good attitude. Such an absence of order and direction leads to insecurity through a lack of predictability—as we have previously discussed.

Because of our large family, I worried more about making room for people than room for things, so I tried to keep clutter to a minimum. Kitchen counters were kept free, save for a decorative plant or some such item. Even small appliances had a home somewhere in the cupboards where they were out of sight, and therefore out of mind until needed. Part of this approach was psychological. When living in quarters smaller than you need, if you can create the perception of space you have gone a long way to relieving a sense of congestion. When we clear the surfaces in the home we help reduce the overload of stimuli in the environment. I developed a habit of not purchasing an item until I had decided in my mind where I would put it when I got home. That saved me some money as well.

We tackled the problem of limited closet space and drawer space by cleaning and sorting all such storage areas on a regular basis. We tried not to keep anything we did not need and endeavored to simplify wherever possible. I remember one June when we were in the Midwest while my husband was completing some university studies, I cajoled the children into helping me reorganize and clean all the closets in the house. On the calendar it was the longest day of the year, and I promised that if they would hang in there with me on this project for as long as the light lasted, then when the shortest day of the year arrived in December we would have a read-a-thon and eat chocolates. They responded beyond my expectations and we worked all day. Unfortunately, when December rolled around we belatedly realized we had forgotten that school would be in session on the shortest day of the year, and our original plan had to be adjusted. However, I do not think any of the children regretted the long day we spent organizing our environment and working together that summer.

Individual families bring about order in ways that work for them, depending on their own particular circumstances. I have been interested to see some of the methods that have helped families stay organized. For example, some have each person clear their own plates and silverware after a meal and take them to the kitchen counter—or even have each person rinse their dishes and place them in the dishwasher. What a great idea! Unfortunately, we did not have a dishwasher for most of the time our children were growing up (just dish washers with dishpan hands), and there were so many plates, utensils, and so forth, the table clearer needed to have a stacking plan or the counter would have overflowed. But the point here is that there is no one way for taking care of the details of maintaining order—only that it happens. I have found many things that worked for others would not work for me due to the size of our family. Where some mothers train their children to handle their own laundry (which I think is admirable) I found that impractical. With so many vying for the washer and dryer we would have had scheduling conflicts; and many small loads were not as thrifty as fewer large loads in terms of water, power, and detergent. So, I trained the children how to do laundry using family loads. "Whatever works" is the mantra here.

One of the nice benefits of keeping order in a large family is the practical necessity of eating together. The kitchen could not have stood the mess of having everyone cooking and snacking independently throughout the day; so we fixed three meals a day, ate together, and reaped all the benefits of meeting around the table. Exceptions were made, of course, for those working late or unable to be home for meals. Other families may have different routines that serve them well, but eating together is a worthy goal.

Making the environment work for a family includes more than simply controlling our material surroundings. We also need to be aware of noise levels. Our ears are frequently bombarded by an overload of stimuli, which can reduce our peace and effectiveness just as readily as too much clutter and visual stimuli. Children are not only messy; they are noisy—and that is fine. From the infant's first babbles, which delight us, to the funny jokes our teenagers tell, we rejoice in communicating with our children. Nevertheless, the decibel level needs to be considered, and in our family I continually encouraged people to lower voices when they became too loud. I tried to set the standard by not yelling or raising my voice. In addition to a more peaceful environment, I knew that if the children were used to hearing me speak in low tones, and I ever needed to get their attention in an emergency or for an important reason, I could raise my voice and count on them listening to me. Loud voices should be the exception, not the rule.

Closely connected to the suggestion of lowering the volume level in the home is the idea of keeping the conversation pleasant. In addition to the good manners evident in such words as "please," "thank you," and "excuse me," it is helpful to request rather than demand, inquire rather than interrogate, remind rather than blame. Words are powerful and therefore should be used with care. We should use no words that belittle or disparage another, and should allow no derogatory nicknames. If we use unflattering words to label a child we stand the chance they may believe us. Elder Jeffrey R. Holland reminds us: "Be constructive in your comments to a child—always. Never tell them, even in whimsy, that they are fat or dumb or lazy or homely. You would never do that maliciously, but they remember and may struggle for years trying to forget—and to forgive."[1]

It is also important to remember that considerate speech goes far beyond word choice; the tone of voice is perhaps even more important. I learned as a young mother that if I were at all impatient or distraught when I picked up a baby after he or she had awakened from a nap I could expect the baby to be more difficult to deal with throughout the afternoon, emotions being very contagious. If, on the other hand, I smiled and spoke in a gentle, loving voice, regardless of how my day had been to that point, I could set the tone for the next few hours. At that age words carry no meaning and tone of voice is everything—I could call them little bothersome rascals and they would not care as long as I smiled and spoke lovingly.

As children grow the meanings of words matter, but the tone of voice can soften the message and make it easier to be received. Many times I corrected one of the children when they had spoken harshly or unkindly, and often I would get a reply something like this: "But Mom, it's their fault. They told me they wouldn't wear my stuff unless they asked me." I would usually reply that I understood the issue, but there was a kinder way to say it. How many times have we reminded a child to ask nicely? It is not that the message should not be delivered, rather that it should be done in a way that is not hurtful. A well-known proverb reminds us, "A soft answer turneth away wrath: but grievous words stir up anger" (Proverbs 15:1). This is certainly true in family life. Part of our job description as parents is to teach and correct, but we can do much to show our children how to communicate kindly when we are careful with our own choice of words and tone of voice. Requiring our children to respect one another can only be done when we show the same respect for each one of them.

By lowering the intensity of the discourse we avoid the problem of escalation. It is easy to try to "go one better" when in a contentious conversation. When the volume gets louder and louder, the body language more dramatic, and the words less respectful, the original cause of contention may grow in magnitude. To counter this tendency, it is wise to maintain an attitude of quiet reasonableness, perhaps even understatement, as we keep the conversation based on reality rather than emotion.

It would be hard to leave the problem of assaults on the ear without giving some consideration to the sounds coming from electronic and media sources. Added to the voices of family members and multiple friends are the TV, radio, CD player, DVDs, and other electronics. There were times when I would sense something bothering me and upon further reflection realize it was noise pollution. From most rooms in the house emanated competing electronic sounds. I have decided most teenagers go through a stage when the current popular music needs to accompany them wherever they are. Thus, the portable boom box, or the MP3 player (or current favorite device) moves from kitchen to bedroom to bathroom—where even a shower needs musical accompaniment. Altogether, it constituted a racket that held hostage the family members who craved silence, or at least less clamor. I would make my rounds asking that volume be lowered or that the music be given a time-out. It was not that music was unwelcome, and we were fortunate not to have to counter hard rock and other particularly jarring genres, but too many sources playing too loudly was unwelcome.

Music, with some supervision, can be a wonderful part of family life. A rousing song can keep the work moving along during chore time. For some reason one of our favorite tapes to accompany cleaning the kitchen was of stirring, patriotic songs. Piano playing was a frequent backdrop to family living, and scheduling time for four or more children to get in practice time took some organization. Others might have been practicing the trumpet or some other instrument—or *should* have been. It was an ongoing struggle to get children to practice, but I never tired of hearing the practice sessions themselves. In fact, sometimes the music would really ring through the house. On one occasion a son was preparing a trumpet solo for state competition and his sister was going to be his accompanist. However, the piano accompaniment was so complex and fast it was very difficult to play; so we were treated to weeks of magnificent music as the two teenagers worked to perfect the piece.

Whether a child chooses to make music, or any other talent, an important part of his life is an individual matter. Some of my children wanted it enough to practice. Others chose other interests, equally worthwhile. It is fortunate, for the good of our society, that our talents and interests are not all alike. What is important in this framework is that life needs to be so ordered that individuals are given the opportunity to choose wherever possible. For example, we required that all of the children have basic instruction in music so they would have the benefit of such exposure, and they would then have some basis upon which to decide whether music was something they wanted to pursue. This was a personal choice for our family, and it may not be the right one for another. Yet, it is important that each family decide what does matter to them and then organize the household to make those things possible.

I wish we had come closer to the ideal of order through the years. It helped a great deal to work toward it, and we would have been in an impossible mire had we not; but it rarely all came together. I remember a frustrated entry in my journal about not being able to put my hand on a pen when I needed it, or scissors, or whatever I needed. There were too many little people playing school or Primary who could not remember to put things back where they belonged.

One of our sorest points was getting everyone to bed at night. We were largely successful with the younger children, but the teenagers would frequently stay up late despite repeated counsel and reminders. We never really solved the issue. Sometimes I think they have to learn by the consequences they suffer the next day as they drag through the afternoon tired and out of sorts. I do know our efforts made a difference, and that is the reward that comes from working to achieve order.

I wish to conclude this section on order by discussing two closely related topics: cleanliness and beauty. Having a clean and attractive home is one of our goals as homemakers, and it is important that we recognize that order is a prerequisite to making that happen.

Cleanliness was something I worked at every day, and rarely achieved. There was too much to do and too little time. I grew up in an immaculate home and liked that standard to be the way I lived my life. However, as the family grew, it became harder and harder to maintain my surroundings, and I became frustrated and discontent at times. After a particularly trying day, I dreamed that I was in a mess with my living room floor knee-deep in clutter, and that the doorbell rang and upon answering it I found the CBS Anchorman, Dan Rather, on my doorstep. Oh! The horror! So, I struggled to keep up, and when I expressed my concern to my husband that I just could not maintain my standard any more, he wisely suggested I lower it. He could be counted on to give me help whenever he could, and I knew his advice was good. Instead of trying to scour the entire kitchen at one time, I would clean one cupboard while I was watching dinner simmer on the stove. Rather than trying to keep everything as neat as a pin all day, I aimed to get everything where it belonged at least once in a twenty-four-hour period. I learned the value of five or ten minutes. If I hustled full tilt I could transform a room in that amount of time, and transform my outlook at the same time.

Though it required continual effort to keep things orderly and clean, I knew this was the pattern we were trying to follow. As the Lord instructed, "Set in order your houses; keep slothfulness and uncleanness far from you" (D&C 90:18). Efforts made to make home a clean and inviting place would be rewarded.

During these times of feeling overwhelmed, I reminded myself of what I have always known to be true: People matter more than things. Children matter more than our need to keep up on the housework. So, yet again, we come back to the basic premise of this work: do what is best for the child. We cannot forget that doing what is right for children does not mean giving them what they want at the expense of Mother or other members in the family; it is in the best interest of children to understand that everyone in the family counts. In this situation, however, we are considering the welfare of the child in relationship to her surroundings.

In the larger scheme of things, we know it is good for a child to have a structured, clean, and neat environment, and it is worth working toward. Yet, some needs of children may temporarily supersede that worthy goal. Their needs for love, attention, security, and stimulation can never be neglected. This truth reminds us to add the qualifier to our premise: do what is right for the child in the moment. At any particular point in the day it may be more important to cuddle a baby, read to a toddler, help a preschooler finish a puzzle, or decorate a birthday cake. Sometimes the day-to-day chores will just have to wait because there is living to be done.

We all need a measure of beauty in our lives. Some interesting research has been done showing that health and happiness are impacted depending on whether we receive positive or negative inputs from the world around us. All our senses funnel messages into our consciousness. This is why we avoid harshness, disorder, ugliness, and disharmony, and seek for an atmosphere which provides an uplifting ambiance. Providing a home where both body and spirit can be refreshed is our objective. We, like many others, cannot afford beautiful paintings and expensive décor, so it is comforting to know that the concepts of order and cleanliness, already mentioned, will do more to give us pleasant surroundings than anything else we can do—and they are free. If I ever became discouraged because I could not afford to redo or update, I would spring clean and rearrange the furniture for a fresh look.

There are, however, some things that can be done to improve our surroundings on a small budget. I remember my sister once noting that everyone has to paint their walls and since a gallon of paint costs the same no matter what color it is, we might as well make a good choice. We do make choices all the time and, whether we are replacing wall color, flooring or furniture, we can obey the laws of harmony and style. Color has personality and can be used to make a positive difference in our surroundings. Smaller transformations can be made using throws, cushions, potted plants, and muted lighting. There are touches of refinement that most of us can manage. I tried to have a cloth on the table, even for mealtimes. It meant more laundry, but a well-set table with serving bowls instead of pans, for example, lends graciousness to even plain food. Like everyone, we had days where we were grateful just to get everyone fed and could not worry about the niceties, but generally it is worth the effort to create a pleasant, mannered eating environment. I recall as a child my mother making many a rancher's cabin homey through her gracious touch. One time we all accompanied my father to Montana for three weeks where we lived in a ghost town. That was a wonderful adventure, but it meant finding a cabin that had not yet fallen down in order to set up temporary living quarters. It did not take long to settle in with our limited possessions before we were out looking for wildflowers to grace the old, splintery table Mother had covered with a cloth.

In instances where a harsh overhead light reveals too many imperfections, merely adding muted lighting with lamps will make the surroundings mellower. Again, we are dealing with perceptions. If a room is appealing and has harmony and balance, a person entering will feel comfortable and at home. Many women are talented crafters and bring color and personality into their homes and, surely, many of the fun and rewarding times in homemaking occur when our creative juices flow and we fashion an item that will make a nice change or addition to our home.

I think, however, we need to remind ourselves when speaking of our physical surroundings that these are only things. People will always matter more. If our choice is between giving our time to our children and decorating our home beautifully, we must ascertain what is right for that child and do that—and such a decision will always be a personal one. If monetary resources are tight, and we cannot afford the nice accoutrements without leaving the home to work, we need to be reassured that order and cleanliness are free . . . and they are enough.

Work

Another very important part of the training we parents give our children is that of teaching them to work. I feel such concern regarding this aspect of child rearing, I hesitate in broaching the subject for fear it will run away with me and I will not know where to stop. Being able to work is one of the most vital attributes necessary for a lifetime of service and success, and yet it is becoming one of the most neglected. This message has been expressed by our prophets: "Children must be taught to work at home. They should learn there that honest labor develops dignity and self-respect. They should learn the pleasure of work, of doing a job well."[2] As many times as we have been told by our leaders, and as much as we know intuitively that work is good for us, we tend to reduce it to an increasingly smaller role in the lives of our children.

Because of a changing society, the demands on our youth have changed as well. With our present lifestyle there is often not enough meaningful work to do, and well-meaning parents puzzle over that problem. We assign some household chores, but in terms of time and effort they do not amount to much. We do not want our children parked in front of the television or playing video games for hours on end, so we try to fill their lives with constructive alternatives. We sign them up for sports, gymnastics, dance, violin lessons, swimming lessons, and on and on. These are all good activities, but they are not work and they are all about the child. This evolving tendency to focus a child's activities and thoughts on himself is one I would like to return to at a later time, but first I wish to make a few points regarding the role of work in a child's life.

Knowing how to work has obvious practical implications. We certainly want our children to learn how to take care of themselves and their future families; to make a living, where necessary; and to willingly contribute to the world in a meaningful way. To do all of these things well, children need to learn and practice an array of skills. With this in mind we encouraged our children to develop as many skills as possible, and over time the list became quite lengthy—partly because of our need to do as much for ourselves as we were able.

We were careful not to promote artificial, gender-specific roles. Rather we encouraged each child, male or female, to learn a wide variety of skills in the home and family setting. For example, everyone was expected to do some "unfun" things such as shelling nuts and weeding. Eventually, however, interest and proficiency exerted themselves and the girls became better at cutting and styling hair, sewing, and cooking from scratch, whereas the boys excelled with car care and outdoor work. When my mother first married my rancher father, her new mother-in-law advised my mother never to learn to milk a cow. I thought that was good advice as well, so we happily let the boys, under their father's guidance, develop and use that skill on their own.

It has previously been mentioned that self-confidence comes from being self-sufficient and able to do many things well. The heart of self-esteem is the ability to be of use in a meaningful way. In the research pertaining to large acts of altruism, where someone goes to the aid of another at the peril of her own life, it has been shown that a person is more likely to try to help another in an emergency situation if she has the capability of doing so. An individual is more likely to jump into a swollen stream to rescue a drowning person if he knows how to swim.

Having the tools and knowledge with which to work is enabling, and the more capabilities a person has, the more confidence he is likely to have, and the more likely he is to render assistance in that way.

I am reminded, in this context, of an instance one of our sons reported to us in one of his letters home while he was serving a foreign mission. He and his companion were having dinner at the home of a member family in the area, when it was explained to them that if they needed to use bathroom facilities, they would need to use public accommodations some distance away because the toilet in the apartment had been out-of-order for over a year. My son replied that he knew something about toilets and would be happy to have a look at it. He quickly ascertained that only a small, inexpensive part was necessary for the repair and he had the toilet in working order before the evening was over. Now that may not be a large act of altruism, but I'm sure the family members were grateful they no longer had to leave their apartment every time they needed a toilet. Having some simple, basic knowledge of plumbing made our son serviceable. This missionary son may not have particularly enjoyed learning the plumbing trade as he worked with his father and brothers to keep the aging system in our older home working, but he was glad he had that knowledge when he was able to help someone far from home. The more we know, the better equipped we are to help. The boys may never need to know how to milk a cow in the future—but then again they might!

The self-confidence that comes from being able to work and do many things leads to our use of initiative and independence. Such creativity should be encouraged in our children. We want them to be able to take what they know and build upon it using their own talents and initiative. Let me give an example. Though I tried each school day to have dinner well-planned and underway before the children got home from school, there were times when that did not happen. On occasions when I needed help with dinner, I would ask one of the girls to handle it for me. Usually she would ask what she was supposed to fix. Often I had not had time to give it much thought, and I would suggest she just see what we had in the refrigerator, freezer, fruit room, and cupboards, and then use her own ingenuity. This was the challenge: do the best you can with what you have. If I had not been grocery shopping for a while, that may have been quite a challenge, but the dinner cook always came through, and often with a tasty meal. Teaching children to define the objective of a task, assess what the environment can provide, and then achieve the goal is important knowledge to pass on.

Allowing children to build on their learning requires mothers (and fathers) to give up some control and learn to trust them. The boys in our family had various interests through the years and we tried to give them as free a rein as possible because we knew they were learning as they worked. At one point in time two of the boys were in the chicken business. One day I walked into the living room to see the boys and a hundred baby chicks in the middle of the floor. Since one of the house rules was not to have animals in the house, I was somewhat surprised. They quickly assured me they had fully protected the carpet and hemmed them in, but that it was necessary to have the chicks at hand because the little chicks did not have their hen moms to peck the hardened feces off their little bums, and they would die if they could not excrete their waste. So here were the preteen boys, carefully cleaning the rear end of each chick with Q-tips. How could I protest when they had done their research and were working so diligently? Eventually, in this general spirit of progress, the boys decided they did not even have to order baby chicks and could hatch them from eggs, so they researched and then built a large egg hatchery which was very clever in design and worked well.

Sometimes their ingenuity would catch me and their father by surprise. On one occasion when the boys were raising steers, they had their dad put in an order for hay at their expense, but he had over-ordered for their purposes, and not too long after the hay arrived half of it disappeared. When my husband walked out early one morning headed for school, he noticed that half the stack was missing and phoned the police to report the theft. Our good neighbor from across the street remarked that it was nice of the thief to take only half the stack and then to go the extra mile by carefully covering the remaining hay with the tarp. As it turned out, the boys had found a buyer for the surplus hay and were recovering some of their money.

I later quizzed my husband on why he had not automatically suspected the boys were tending to their business, because by then I had learned to expect the unexpected. One time I went out to the car only to find that the radio and players had been removed. Never once did I suspect that the electronics had been stolen. I merely asked one of the electronics-minded sons, the next time I saw him, when I might expect to have the equipment restored. He was experimenting to try and improve the system and it was not long before it was back where it belonged and working perfectly (though I do not know that it was improved). It would have been counterproductive to have discouraged such interest. Today these curious electronic buffs are techno-wizards.

Sometimes the best thing we parents can do is get out of the way and just try to manage the mess. One season the boys were raising bummer lambs. They built a portable, floorless pen they could move from place to place around the yard so the lambs could forage on the lawn and other spring grasses. The wire pen was about five feet by five feet in dimension and we soon had five-by-five foot brown spots everywhere. I had to weigh carefully whether a nice, well-kept yard mattered more than the boys. The boys won out. Sometime later they were into bicycles and we had about thirty bikes around in various stages of completeness. They would make one good bike out of a number of "well-used" bicycles, and learned much in the process. In this case I did suggest the disorder be confined to one area.

As they grew, the learning curve grew steeper. Bicycle repair turned into motorcycle repair and eventually into auto mechanics—and we were still trying to accommodate the resulting untidiness (I came to appreciate that creativity needs some disorder to flourish). I well remember looking out of a second story window at the yard one day when it looked like a tornado had just gone through. In this project the boys had a truck they were repainting and fenders, bumpers, hood and trunk parts, and other miscellany, were spread over a wide area. I expressed my concern to them about being unable to water the lawn, but with multiple coats of paint being applied, we just had to be patient. Eventually, the finished product was admired and the lawn restored, but most important the boys knew a whole lot more than when they began the project.

Though we may carefully teach the process of doing something, there comes a time when we have to allow for trial and error, hands-on learning. Since baking and cooking were done on a fairly large scale in our household, I trained many kitchen helpers, but we still ate some "unusual" fare as the budding cooks practiced. Only when something was unsalvageable, like the time one of the girls interchanged the cocoa with the flour in a chocolate cake recipe, did we throw the creation out. Another time one of the teenagers was going to treat us to a new culinary treat she had just learned about. She was trying to heat a can of sweetened condensed milk in order to carmelize it so it could be served as a yummy fruit dip, when we heard a mini-explosion. We did not get a chance to eat that experiment because it was all over the ceiling, the cabinets, and the floor.

My mentioning the last incident brings up the important issue of safety. With so much applied learning taking place, how do parents ensure everyone's safety? The answer is that there is no way to ensure that nothing will ever go wrong, but it is important to do all you can to prevent accidents, and part of the training process is to learn safe ways of doing things. Though my husband was a teacher by profession, he was a builder by way of avocation, and he tried to teach the children the same safe habits his contractor father had taught him. With so many carpentry saws, nail guns, ladders, and other tools in use, it was imperative to exhibit great care and respect for what they could do. Other components of the building trade required the same level of attention, such as working with electricity. It would have been easier to avoid anything related to such work, but that would have meant leaving many needed or fulfilling projects undone. Because the boys learned the home-building trade, they have since been able to do much for themselves and their families, as well as to serve others by repairing roofs and porches and completing other needed projects.

Fortunately we were free from serious accidents, but did have a few minor emergencies. One incident occurred when a son and his cousin were working on automobiles, trying to make one good car out of two that did not run. Somehow our son caught his finger on something and almost cut the tip of that finger off. The fingertip was sewn back on and no sign of the accident remains other than a faint scar. On occasion they had close calls. For a number of years one of our sons had been trying to get a combination motorcycle/trailer to work. He had tried all kinds of fixes and experiments. One day I looked out the window and saw him flying down the road perched on the seat of this interesting rig, with a large group of neighborhood kids and siblings supplying the forward momentum by pushing it from behind. It was kind of funny to see this "Tom Sawyer" type of persuasion in action, but it was not as funny when he was on the second level of our property some time later and the throttle stuck. He lost control of the machine and it hurtled over the edge and crashed into the garbage cans below. Fortunately, he bailed off just before it went over and was unhurt. The bottom line is safety will always be an issue, but we learn safety just as we learn everything else. This is one reason we pray night and morning. We use our best judgment, apply appropriate safety measures, and leave the rest up to the Lord.

One last comment on work may be useful. Sometimes we work and we have our children work because it just needs to be done, rather than because it is contributing to a growing body of experience and knowledge. It may be hard, sweaty, tiring work. It may test our stamina and our will. Perhaps we just need the money a heavy labor job can bring in, or need to save money by doing the work ourselves. Through the years we experienced many such times. Corrin secured himself and family members work wherever he could because we needed to supplement his earnings. He and the boys sweated in the fields building and repairing fences, clearing rock, or doing any one of many other difficult and dirty tasks. The summer days were long, and they grew tired, but they did not stop until the workday was complete.

What might be the reward of heavy labor? I think the answer is a simple one: it is just plain good for us. Its physical nature increases our strength and endurance. We learn a lot about ourselves. We learn not to have false pride regarding menial chores we will not "lower" ourselves to do. Honest, hard labor is always honorable. We learn we are not quitters, that we can endure discomfort and fatigue, and that we can see a job through. Never once did I see the children return home bone tired after a full day of work when they did not feel good about themselves and about the day. There is a feeling of accomplishment that comes from hard work.

An interesting family anecdote fits in here. A few years ago we were a part of a major genetic scientific study due to our having such a large number of family members. One aspect of the study tested each of us for the fat composition in our bodies (a test I did not appreciate).

Naturally, competition developed, particularly among the boys, to see who had the lowest percentage of body fat. Some were working out and some were in sports at the time and considered themselves to be "lean machines," so they were keen to learn the test results. Unexpectedly, the one with the lowest body fat in the family was their father, who had no time for sports and never worked out. They looked at me in amazement and said, "How does he do it?" My reply was simply, "He works."

Formal Education and Learning

In speaking about guidance and training, numerous instances of learning have already been recounted. Yet, much of the instruction described so far could be summarized as skills training. As skills increase and are mastered children are better able to care for themselves, their self-confidence grows, and their opportunities for service increase accordingly. However, we also need to mention other kinds of learning that are very important in a child's life, and the role of mothers in fostering such education.

The time will come when children will receive formal education in a school setting. When it does, the success or failure of the child will depend in large part on the attitude he brings to the experience. It appears trite to suggest that mothers should "instill a love of learning" in their children—but it is still true. Whether students are excited about learning new things and are curious about the world depends in large measure on whether their mother (and father) feels the same way. Certain subjects may be more or less appealing than others to any one individual, but the idea of learning something new should be an exciting one to all of us. Corrin is very interested in the natural world of plants and animals, where I am more interested in why people do the things they do. Nevertheless, I can marvel at the large desert creosote plant he points out to me, which survives during drought by dying down to a tiny sprig in order to conserve water, and he can find interesting the latest heritability studies enlightening the nature/nurture debate in psychological research. We should all have or seek to obtain that sense of wonder.

A mother can read to her children when they are young. She can thereby open their narrow surroundings to a much larger world. Throughout my life I have felt a sense of anticipation and pleasure whenever I have stepped into a library—libraries are such realms of possibility—and trips to the library were among our favorite activities. I spent many hours reading to the children, often rereading the same favorite book. I remember a new son-in-law being amazed to hear my small three-year-old son reading word-for-word the pages of his little book. I assured this new family member we did not have a child prodigy on our hands; the book was merely memorized.

Once we are hooked on books we never outgrow the delight of reading. I am reminded of my mother reading *Little Women* to my sister and me, and I was happy to read the same book to my girls. Eventually, our children will read to us as they practice reading, and that can be rewarding if we forget the distractions of the moment and engage ourselves in this important exchange of roles. Not only will our children learn to read, but we will form a three-way connection between the mother, the child, and the story. Stories are so much better shared. My husband's mother is one hundred years old as I write this, and I picture in my mind the way he reads to her now. I am aware, once more, of how shared reading brings us together, whatever our ages. That is one of those great side benefits that comes with this kind of learning.

Beyond the realm of books, we can do much to bring the excitement of learning into our homes. From time to time we would create scheduled learning activities. I remember an autumn season when Corrin gave the children (the oldest being in middle school at the time) a little mini-lesson at breakfast each day before school. He covered a broad range of subjects during those early morning sessions. One day my father visited us unexpectedly, and was surprised to find that Corrin had taught the children the Pythagorean Theorem before school that morning. I do not know how many of the children can explain that theorem today (I would certainly not like to be tested on it), but there is no doubt they picked up on the excitement their father felt about learning. The thrill of knowing something they had never known before was likely the most valuable outcome of those mini-tutorials.

The learning experiences available to family members will be unique to the environment in which they live. For us, we had the desert flora and fauna flourishing in our locale. In order to capitalize on our distinctive surroundings, there was a black bag in our freezer (into which I learned never to reach my hand) that contained frozen specimens of dead creatures, from reptiles to birds of prey. Whenever Corrin would come across dead birds and other animals (never killing for this purpose, as he valued animal life), he would select the best of these remains to use as teaching tools. Our neighbor, a field officer for the state Division of Wildlife Resources, helped expand our knowledge of the natural world by explaining the features of the different snakes, birds, desert tortoises, and other animals he was transporting to new homes (on one occasion it was a black bear). Sometimes we would try to identify scat (droppings) on our hikes, or get up in the middle of the night to witness meteor showers or the reentry of a shuttle. Though I was not always enthusiastic about these nature studies, such as the growing collection of tarantulas, I liked how they served to keep the children curious.

For other families, their surroundings may be very different from the one we experienced, but every family lives in a stimulating environment; and every environment can be a source of curiosity and learning for young minds. We had open space, but we did not have galleries and museums; we had scenic grandeur, but we experienced fewer artistic or cultural events than many cities provide. At the time we were rearing our family, we had friends who were home schooling their children in the East, using the Smithsonian Institute as a classroom and the Kennedy Space Center for a field trip. Each environment has something to offer and the world provides so much to learn, there is never a chance of running out of interesting things to know. For example, our years in China put us on a steep learning curve as we discovered that land with its captivating landscape and fascinating people. Giving children a sense of wonder and curiosity is a priceless gift mothers can bestow.

As children proceed through their school years they will be exposed to volumes of knowledge through books and teachers, and encounter great ideas, some not-so-great ideas, and almost unlimited information. Sometimes they will be excited to learn something new; other times they may be tired, distracted, or bored. Even if we have created a learning climate in our homes, we cannot expect our children to always be delighted at the prospect of hours of homework, studying for exams, and early-morning classes. There have always been enticements to draw students away from their learning tasks. Years ago it might have been the lure of the fishing pond or the building of a tree house. Today it may be going to the mall, getting on the Internet, or watching television.

In this vein I am reminded of the last year we taught in China. I found it curious that freshmen in that university were not permitted to have a personal computer. When I inquired as to the reason for such a restriction, it was explained that the university loses a portion of the freshman class each year due to the playing of computer games. The students become addicted to playing and cannot keep up with their schoolwork. This is such a surprising obsession considering what these students go through to get where they are. This university is one of the top two universities in China; it is considered a great honor to be admitted there. Over 90 percent of China's students never get an opportunity to attend any college or university whatsoever. The students who are granted admittance to a top university have undergone years of intensive study and grueling competition, and their parents and grandparents have sacrificed uncommonly in order to help their sons or daughters achieve this distinction. For these students to lose their future to such a temptation is disheartening.

Mothers are the monitors in the home, and it falls largely to them to guide and protect young minds from the time-wasters (even life-wasters) found in any society. Mothers should take very seriously the potentially damaging effects of the overabundance of electronic gadgetry and stimuli. Sometimes the power has to go out before we realize the peace we are missing. Our family had this reality confirmed one February when we hiked through thigh-deep snow, pulling our gear on a sled, to reach a cabin in the Wyoming Mountains where we spent a week without power and modern conveniences. The first night we were there, it grew dark before we were well situated, so we went to bed early in order to stay warm. As we settled into our beds in the sleeping loft of the cabin, we were uncertain what to do with this unexpected quiet time; it was so dark and so silent. Even our jokes and laughter sounded overly loud in our ears. Our days were filled with building snow forts, melting snow for water, helping one another manage the icy slope to the outhouse, and playing board games in the lamplight. We were unhooked and disentangled from contemporary society's electronic lures, and it helped us view the world through different eyes.

It might serve mothers well to notice how many hours a day their children are either on the phone, online, playing electronic games, watching television, hooked to a music source, or texting their friends. Beyond noticing, we also need to accept the responsibility to limit electronic exposure and establish firm guidelines for the use of electronics.

Not only must we consider the waste of time engendered by too much electronic interference, we worry about the negative images, sounds, and lyrics introduced into the lives of our children. Elder M. Russell Ballard admonishes us, "In the virtual reality and the perceived reality of large and small screens, family-destructive viewpoints and behavior are regularly portrayed as pleasurable, as stylish, as exciting, and as normal. Often media's most devastating attacks on family are not direct or frontal or openly immoral. Intelligent evil is too cunning for that, knowing that most people still profess belief in family and in traditional values. Rather the attacks are subtle and *amoral*—issues of right and wrong don't even come up."[3] In the best interest of our children, we should guide them to choose carefully what they tune into, if they are to avoid an education in evil we do not want them to have.

Just as we learned to do with small children, we can often distract our older children with better options. However, we must not create in them the expectation of being continually entertained. We can assist them in putting their idle time to good use—to accomplish worthy goals, or to perform a service for someone else. We can protect children from becoming ensnared in less meaningful pursuits if we help them be wise stewards of their time.

Even if students have achieved a good balance in their lives, they are not always enlightened scholars, seeking and appreciating knowledge. They may grumble and complain about classes, teachers, subjects, and assignments. That is one of the ways we know they are normal kids. How many parents have had the experience of a child declaring emphatically that she will never use algebra, and cannot see the sense in laboring over that useless subject? The best antidote to such attitudes is to help children gain a comprehensive view of education.

There are actually two visions of education children need to understand. The first one is the need to understand the world we live in and how to be a part of it in a meaningful and fulfilling way. This requires a reservoir of general knowledge. They need a basic understanding of history, geography, peoples, cultures, climates, and global challenges in order to be good citizens of their nation and the world. They would do well to understand the society they live in, its economy, government, rules of law, and societal issues, so they can vote knowledgably and make positive differences wherever they are able. They need to know how the natural world works, and how mankind has changed it for both good and ill. All of these endeavors require a level of acquaintance with language, literature, mathematics, science, the arts, and other basics.

Let me illustrate this universal need to understand the world with another example from my experience in China. One year I was teaching faculty members at the University of Nanjing. Our subject was improving teaching methodologies in the classroom and I was using a wide variety of examples to illustrate the points I was making. In one instance I was using the processes of mitosis and meiosis to demonstrate a particular lesson, only to see a vacant look in the eyes of my students. I prompted them to remember their basic biology classes so they could follow me. Their reply went something like this: "But, Dr. Janice [in China the first and last names are reversed], biology was not our major." These were some of China's brightest and most educated teachers, whom I liked and respected a great deal. I came to understand that a broad-based general education was not required of university students in that country in the same way we experience it here. Biology was not my major either, but I am grateful to have had exposure to the basics of that science.

When I encourage my own children to embrace a broad education, I recommend they strive to be able to hold an intelligent conversation in as many subjects as possible. Not only will they be better citizens of the world, as previously mentioned, they will enjoy life more. Knowledge brings awareness. It is common when we learn a new word to find it cropping up frequently thereafter. The word's rate of occurrence has not changed, but our awareness has. If we are alive to the world around us, we will enjoy it more. We know one of the purposes for the creation of our beautiful and fascinating earth is for our enjoyment, for the Lord has said: "Yea, all things which come of the earth, in the season thereof, are made for the benefit and the use of man, both to please the eye and to gladden the heart; Yea, for food and for raiment, for taste and for smell, to strengthen the body and to enliven the soul" (D&C 59:18–19).

The second vision of education is less general in application than the first, and refers more to our individual requirements for learning. We each have a personal mission to complete on this earth, and each will require a specific set of skills and knowledge in order to do so. The vision, then, is to get the explicit training necessary to accomplish our unique mission here on the earth. Since our assignment will differ from others, our preparations will differ as well. Farmers need an expertise quite different from that of emergency medical technicians; accountants will take different classes from metallurgists. Even within a common field of study, the range of concentration may narrow as the proficiency expands. For example, within the general field of psychology, I focused on social/personality psychology and refined my subject matter further to examine in detail the concept of altruism.

As our children examine their own interests and abilities, they can be guided to choose an area in which they can be happy and successful. Their choice will determine what kinds of preparation they will need. I recall an occasion when a high school son said to me, "I hope just because you and Dad have PhDs you don't expect us children to get one, because I'm sure not going to." My reply was that, of course, we expect no such thing. What we did expect is that he, and his brothers and sisters, would get the tools and knowledge they needed in order to accomplish well their life's work. If a degree is unnecessary for our children to use their full potential in serving others in their chosen vocation or profession, then there is no requirement to get one. There is nothing sacrosanct about a degree. It is difficult but possible to be self-educated, and there are many who have built up wonderful reservoirs of knowledge due to their own diligence. Yet in many professions, degrees are a necessary prerequisite to service. Society has to have ways of measuring proficiency; therefore, certificates, diplomas, or other credentials may be required to enable a son or daughter to do what he or she desires to do. President Gordon B. Hinckley said, "I am not suggesting that all of you should become professional men. What I am suggesting is this: whatever you choose to do, train for it. Qualify yourselves."[4] That is the idea here; we need to help our children prepare to make the best possible contribution in whatever vocation or career they select.

Though a college education may or may not be needed for a particular preparation, it should be noted that it can contribute significantly to the body of general knowledge spoken of earlier. In fact, it is difficult to imagine being well educated without having some college experience. Having access to scientific laboratories and knowledgeable teachers improves and speeds education for most of us. Exposure to competing theories and to multiple perspectives elicits independent and creative thought. Clearly, we can look at learning and at degrees as two different things. All of us need learning; some of us need degrees. I do not recall lecturing our children on getting an education beyond high school; it was merely assumed. We knew that some college experience would be beneficial for them, whether they became college graduates or not. We held the assumption in our home that they would all continue their education beyond high school.

They have varied in the educational pathways they have taken to date, but I hope that learning will be a lifelong endeavor for each one. As an interesting postscript: the son who maintained he would never follow the educational pattern of his parents is now a young PhD. Over time, he realized he needed that level of credential if he were to offer his best to his chosen profession.

The matter of selecting a lifelong career and procuring the necessary preparations for such work sounds easy, but in reality can be very difficult to achieve. Once again, we paint an ideal and then approximate it to the best of our ability. There will be stops and starts, attempts and failures, progress and disappointment. Our children may not know what they want to do. We live in an age of possibilities; our choices are many. They may daydream of being rock stars, sports heroes, or runway models. Keeping these young people focused on the good they can do with their lives, and less interested in personal fame and wealth, will help to center them. As mothers, we are instrumental in providing an exposure to numerous career choices and we can encourage our children to explore many options. We can help them to become self-aware so they can ponder their likes and dislikes, their aptitudes, and their reality-based probabilities for success.

Importantly, mothers need to be aware themselves of the capacities of each of their children. Gifts, talents, and interests vary widely, and the ways in which children learn can differ as well. Psychologists no longer speak in terms of a general IQ. Too much information is lost by such a narrow summation of ability. The brain is so complex, we now speak of multiple intelligences. Some children struggle with reading, but are gifted musicians; some individuals sense intuitively how to get along with others, but may not get along with numbers. Traditional classroom expectations usually require verbal and mathematical competence, and, to an important extent, knowing how to read is elementary to opening up the world; but not all children learn well in visual and auditory ways. Some children who struggle with the verbally-rich curriculum in our schools are transformed when something they can manipulate is placed in their hands. They learn better using their hands-on, kinesthetic intelligence. Let me give an illustration.

When I was commuting from classes one day with another mother who was also in college, she was relating the problems she had had in her sewing class earlier in the day. The teacher had been teaching her students to make pleats by carefully measuring and pinning the folds of the fabric using a marking board and other measuring tools. My friend, however, could not seem to grasp how this was to be done, in spite of the teacher's repeated efforts to demonstrate it to her. It was only when my friend lifted the fabric off the table into her hands that she was able to quickly and deftly form perfect pleats in the air. I laughingly told her she had a wonderful right brain. I, on the other hand, would be lost if the fabric ever left the marked board. We, as mothers, can serve a child well if we can help him identify the talents that are expressly his. In order to do this we need to know our children, their strengths and weaknesses, both in terms of their abilities, as well as their tendencies. Brigham Young admonished us to, "study their dispositions and their temperaments, and deal with them accordingly."[5]

Throughout the formal education process, students may need to change and adapt as they move forward; but all need to persevere. Just as we teach our children to labor long hours in sweaty manual labor without giving up, we need to help them find the reserves to stay the course in other areas of their lives. Through example, mothers can demonstrate this enduring capacity. We can try to be "on time and on task" each day, and to forge new pathways when old ones are blocked. We cannot be easily discouraged, but need to demonstrate ingenuity and faith in overcoming challenges. Our children will likely look to our example when they encounter a similar test.

Allow me to give an example of this quality. It was an effort for me to overcome some obstacles while getting my education. Several times we moved the family for durations of one year, in order to obtain proximity to the university classes I needed. After serious reflection I felt the moves were a step forward for the children, as they would have new environments and challenges and would grow from the experience. The first time we moved the family for one year, most of the children thought it was a great adventure. However, our son who was to attend ninth grade was reluctant to move away from his friends and projects. I assured him he would have some new experiences he would never be able to have in our present surroundings. Reluctantly, he agreed. By the time we had been in our new location for a few months, he certainly had had some unusual experiences, including having his bike stolen, and outrunning six fellow students he had challenged for cheating in gym class. I told him after those encounters, "See. I was right!" I hoped he could see the humor in the situation. Fortunately, the year was a good one; the children's view of the world was enlarged, and they learned they could make new friends, develop new interests, and enjoy themselves in the process.

In the context of the present discussion, the children also witnessed that it may require extraordinary effort to bring about ordinary progress. This was a tough way to go to school. Moving the entire family for one-year intervals was a major achievement, but even greater sacrifice was sometimes required. Some semesters I would commute several times a week, getting up at three in the morning, driving 250 miles to classes, and then driving 250 miles home the same day. In retrospect I believe it benefited the children to see perseverance demonstrated in this way because getting a college education has not been easy for them, either. It has required planning, hard work, and persistence. One of our daughters married when she had only one quarter remaining before graduating from the University of Utah. She and her new husband moved to Denver where she tried to transfer her credits to another university in that city in order to complete her degree. Because of university policies she was unable to make that happen. So, in another extraordinary effort to complete an ordinary quarter of schooling, she flew by commercial airline every week from Denver to Salt Lake City to attend classes and then flew home again. It may be interesting to note, this was the same daughter who had nightmares about long mouse tails when she was five. Keeping children secure when they are young really does help them become independent adults who are free to choose their educational goals.

Our children do watch us; they see how we respond to difficulties. I wish I had been a better example. Sometimes I got tired or discouraged, and gave up for a while. I would ponder, rethink, regroup, and then move forward. Fortunately, it is the moving forward again that counts. In our mothering, if we can communicate to our children our conviction that knowledge is worth working for, and that it is acquired for the purpose of doing good, and for enjoying the world in which we live, we will have done them a great service.

Obedience

Teaching our children to be obedient is another stewardship we mothers assume as we rear our families. We have good kids—but they're still kids. That means they will not do everything they are supposed to do when they are supposed to do it. We as parents know that teaching obedience is part of our job description, but there are such differing ideas on how this is best done that we can become confused. After reading about discipline in the developmental literature and seeing it administered throughout a lifetime of experience, I think we can summarize in four words what good discipline should be. In a nutshell, discipline should be firm, consistent, appropriate, and loving.

By firm we mean that it should make enough of an impression on a child that he remembers the correction sufficiently to do better next time. If it is trite or meaningless, it may strengthen the behavior we are trying to change rather than modify it. Sometimes mothers feel like they are talking to a wall when they are trying to amend a child's behavior. If children feel free to ignore or laugh at an attempt by Mom to get them to obey, the punishment for the disobedience is not firm enough. Sometimes a mother has to repeat a request over and over in an escalating tone of voice before she can get compliance. In such a situation she is allowing her children to show disrespect for her, and this is not good for the child—thereby running counter to the thesis underlying all mothering.

Though discipline should be firm, it should never be harsh or punitive. We aim to teach compliance with as little distress as possible. My father was very strict and had only to tell us one time to do something before we obeyed. My husband, on the other hand, received a swat on his bottom only once, and that was when he was two years old. He had tipped over a gallon of molasses, and happily spread it around the kitchen floor. I contrast these two examples to illustrate that, though I turned out okay (at least that's how I see myself) with my strict upbringing, so did Corrin, without the use of corporal punishment. Considering that disciplinary measures are not pleasant parts of child rearing, we would like to have those occasions be as few and as mild as possible. If I could do my parenting over, I would be just as firm in my expectations, but softer in my corrections. In this case, less is definitely better. President Gordon B. Hinckley believed in a firm, but gentle approach. "There is no discipline in all the world like the discipline of love. It has a magic all its own."[6] We remind ourselves, yet again, to do what is right for each individual child in the moment, and that may take thought and prayer. President James E. Faust addressed this concern: "One of the most difficult parental challenges is to appropriately discipline children. Child rearing is so individualistic. Every child is different and unique. What works with one may not work with another. I do not know who is wise enough to say what discipline is too harsh or what is too lenient except the parents of the children themselves who love them most. It is a matter of prayerful discernment for the parents."[7] I subscribe to this formulation.

Children need boundaries. With boundaries they feel more secure, and they are safer. But after thirty years of living with children of all ages and sizes, I'm a believer that if parental expectations are clear to children, if they have learned to trust and respect their mother and father, and if they feel loved and respected themselves, they will be naturally inclined to be obedient. The following example illustrates this point. One December, we had a rash of broken glass. One of our sons broke a lovely, decorated mirror in the living room when he was clowning around. Not long after, he accidentally broke a window in his bedroom. To top it off, when one of the boys was outside pitching logs for the fireplace to his brother standing on the deck, one of the pieces of the logs went amiss and broke a sliding glass door. Fortunately for them, we had no three-strikes-and-you're-out rule at our house. The boys really did not even need a lecture on being more careful. As they helped us board-up the broken door to keep out the cold while we had the glass replaced, they knew this circumstance had put a severe strain on our finances. They were not happy to have caused the problem, and I felt sure they would be more careful in the future.

This does not mean there should be no consequences to broken house rules. There definitely should be family policies in force that should be observed. It is just that in the case cited above we had no family rule against such accidents; and as always, people matter more than things. So, it is important for parents to see what is in play at the moment and do the right thing by disciplining appropriately. Smaller children, of course, will need more supervision and training as they learn what constitutes fitting behavior.

I think the concept of consistency, as it relates to the teaching of obedience, is so well acknowledged that our discussion here can be brief. When the rule of consistency is broken, the expectations regarding behavior are lost as well. It will not be clear to children what is expected of them if the behavior is condemned one time and condoned or ignored another, and disobedience will likely increase. The senses of order and predictability that serve children so well break down. This is not to say that justice should not be tempered by mercy at times, but that it should be made clear to the child why this departure from the norm is taking place. This is another one of those areas in which mothering is more an art than a science. If a mother can tell that a lesson has been learned or that a softer response will serve the child better, it is nice to know there is nothing absolute about rules. Rules are here to serve us, not the other way round.

Appropriate discipline refers to "suiting the punishment to the crime," so to speak. A minor infraction of a rule should receive a mild reprimand, and one of greater consequence should receive a commensurate penalty. Additionally, finding a punishment that is a natural consequence of the mistake serves as an effective reminder when the same behavior is considered in the future. Perhaps a child neglects to make her bed or put her toys away, and so has to skip play group in order to get those chores completed. Life has consequences, and we do our children a favor when we teach them to recognize early and consistently the effects of their choices, good or bad.

The fourth point is that we should teach obedience as lovingly as possible, and in a way that our children know we care more about them than we do for the rule. This is why we try to make discipline as gentle and mild as we can manage and still be effective. We avoid a battle of wills whenever possible and tone down the rhetoric when it heats up.

Nevertheless, rules are not fun and they're not likely to win parents any popularity contests. I recall an occasion when one of our daughters, fourteen years old at the time, was upset because her curfew on Friday and

Saturday nights was 10:30 PM. She watched her older brothers and sisters coming in by midnight, and figured she should have the same freedom. To compound her complaint, she informed us that she was the only one of her peers who had to be home so early (the meanest-mother-on-the-block syndrome). She contended that everyone else's parents permitted their daughters much more freedom. Had she been able to persuade us toward a more permissive attitude, she would have felt freer, but more vulnerable. Safety versus freedom is a timeless dilemma, and where children are concerned, a mother needs to weigh the balance between the two very carefully—regardless of whether or not it is a popular position to take.

Even older teenagers need to be protected and must regularly be reminded that their welfare is one of our paramount concerns. One of our house rules was that those who were away for the evening, dating or working, needed to check in with me or my husband upon their return so that we would know they had arrived home safely—and prior to the bewitching hour of midnight. One evening we had a family with young children visiting with us and staying overnight. We had no guest bedroom but did have a large living room that worked well for overnight guests. Unfortunately, to get to the second floor bedroom and bath quarters which our four teenage daughters shared, one had to go through the living room. Two of the girls retired for the night, but the other two were on dates. I dozed off while waiting for their return and when I awakened sometime in the night I realized they had not checked in. Not knowing for sure if they were home, I quietly crept through the living room and tapped lightly on the girls' locked door, so as not to awaken our guests. Naturally, that did not work! It would have taken pounding on the door to rouse those girls, so I returned to where my husband was sleeping and roused him instead. He ended up hauling our tall ladder around to the front of the house where the upstairs bedroom window was located, and he climbed up to knock on the window, hoping no passerby would see him and call the police. He eventually ascertained the girls were safely in their beds—and the girls and I did have a little chat the next morning. Importantly, they never doubted we cared about them.

It is helpful to curtail undesirable behaviors as soon as possible after they manifest themselves. I would like to share a valuable insight as to how this can be done. Too often in a family the atmosphere in the home takes on a negative tone. Generally, this is because one or more of the members of the family has become self-centered. As mothers, if we can change this inward focus by helping children forget about themselves, we can solve the problem. Following are a few examples that demonstrate this idea.

There are rough times in every family when needling, teasing, griping, or other negative expressions predominate. Children may become bored, irritated, or focused on their own needs or wants, and brothers and sisters become barely tolerated annoyances. At times when I could see such general discontent, I knew I could turn the situation around by having the children become productive again, and I would have all of us go outside and work hard on the yard for a couple of hours. They came back in tired, but feeling better about themselves. The yard looked nice, the exercise had invigorated them, and their self-esteem was better because they were useful once again. I had actually changed what they were thinking about. Their focus was no longer on themselves.

Occasionally, if I could see the children were developing the habit of criticizing one another, I would choose a meal when everyone was present and after eating I had each person tell one positive thing about every other person at the table before anyone was excused. This always changed the climate around our home. I remember a home evening especially designed to help the children look for the good in one another. During the week they were to watch for positive things they saw their brothers and sisters do, write it on a piece of paper, and deposit the paper in a container taped to the refrigerator. Some of the entries were so cute I wrote them in my journal, such as the one where one of our little daughters wrote on her note how her big sister, Marianne, brought home (from the store where she worked after school) some pink polka-dot pants for her. The children were no longer focused on the irritating actions they could see in their brothers and sisters, but on the many good things they did for one another.

Other times a well-chosen story or poem helped home evenings work their magic. The children forgot their own concerns when they felt empathy for the struggles and adversities of others. As they considered the sorrows and joys, the failures and successes, the challenges and triumphs of others, their moods softened. Their focus shifted.

It became apparent to me that we can improve the habitual ways a child thinks. When a child becomes less concerned about what he or she wants, and thinks in terms of how to help others, moods and sensitivities alter in a constructive way. In this same vein, uplifting music is another powerful tool for maintaining a kind and optimistic tone in the home.

As was mentioned earlier, it helps to cultivate a sense of humor; it is easier for children to accept correction if the mood is kept light and less intense. Sometimes a funny or clever observation is all they need to see the error of their ways. And many happenings around home really are funny. I remember one time when a middle-school-age son had persuaded his youngest brother to shave off one of his eyebrows. I did not approve, of course, but I struggled not to laugh as I scolded.

That same son, some years later when he was a senior in high school, came bounding up the stairs to our bedroom late one night and stood at the foot of our bed. He announced, "I have to tell you something. You are going to see an extra charge on your credit card bill." It seems he was curious about online bidding and wanted to see how it worked. He needed a credit card in order to follow the process, so he borrowed one of ours. Unfortunately, his was the winning bid on a new scanner. We all laughed at his unintended purchase. Not too long afterward, he traded his labor for a top-of-the-line food dehydrator and gave it to us to make up for the surprise scanner—though no amends were expected or necessary. Laughing is one of the things families do best, and it can take the edge off an otherwise stressful event.

Responsibility

When children are young, we can begin to teach them responsibility for their words and actions. We expect them to keep their toys off the stairs and their tricycles out of the driveway. As children grow older, responsibility increases and they learn to be where they say they will be and do what they say they will do. If they are part of a sports team, they learn to be to the practices and games, as they agreed; that is one of the important benefits of team membership. If a promise is made, it is kept. If a child does not learn to be dependable in a part-time job now, the chances increase that such neglect will impact his employability later.

I am reminded of a time when one of our daughters did not make it on time to a part-time job she held. The store phoned to see if she was planning on coming in to work, and we were surprised because she had intended to leave the outing she was on with her sister and another friend in time to get to work. It was possible, I thought, she had become engrossed in what was happening and had misjudged the time, or even had been thoughtless or careless. However, we worried about her no-show because she had accepted the responsibility of this job and had never been late or careless about it before, so we immediately began to look for her. As it turned out, the teenagers had gone for a ride in a Jeep on a remote, dirt road and had hit a rock submerged in water, tipping over the vehicle. Though they were eventually able to get themselves out of the situation, it was this daughter's reputation for dependability that alerted us to the trouble.

Although our home was on less than half an acre of ground, it was helpful that the local ordinances allowed animals. It made learning responsibility through animal care possible. When the boys first brought bummer lambs home, the young animals needed to be fed by bottle every four hours around the clock, so they asked their older brother if he would awaken them during the night for the feeding. Yet, they remained uneasy, worrying he might forget. Not daring to take the chance those lambs would go hungry, they decided they would take turns staying awake through the night in order to watch the clock. They took forty-five-minute watches with one staying awake while the other slept. When we heard how they were managing this situation, we knew, of course, that system would not work, and their father assured them they could sleep well, because he would awaken them at the right time. We were pleased that they cared about the welfare of their charges, and Corrin did not relieve them of their responsibility by feeding the lambs himself. Rather, he made it possible for two young boys to have this experience in trust-worthiness without endangering their health.

There were always many "creative" ideas floating around our house, and we tried to give the children some freedom in trying them out—with the caveat that they take responsibility for the time, expense, and disorder that might accompany such ventures. Switching rooms, moving furniture, and redesigning their bedroom spaces were common. From sleeping in the playhouse in the backyard, to rigging up a bed in a walk-in closet for the youngest sibling to use (which I did negate), they experimented with their environment.

When one of our youngest daughters had finally gotten a room of her own, she wanted to completely redecorate it. As usual, that was fine by me as long as she bore the expense for anything that could not be used on a permanent basis. In this case, she wanted an African motif and that meant red walls; so she bought the paint, mosquito netting, and other decorative touches, and did all the work. I admired and advised, and paid for the window treatments because they were a needed update. I watched her work, responsibly protect the furniture and carpet, and create for weeks—and the room turned out great. We tried to let the children know from the time they were small that if they could be trusted to be responsible, they would have freedom to take initiative in their lives.

Responsibility applied to the humdrum of daily living as well. We tried to teach that we are each responsible to play a part in making the group we live in work. Whether it is our childhood home, our roommates at college, a companion on a mission, or our marriage partner, we must shoulder our share of the work. In family life there should be no divisions of labor that make some prima donnas and others servants. And, that includes Mother. Though she may be in full-time service to her family, she is not the servant, and her children should be mindful of her needs and care about the quality of her life. We are really doing something in our children's best interest when we require them to treat us well. Our greatest lesson in responsibility is to learn to take care of one another.

Spiritual Education

We mothers know that providing guidance to our offspring in the realm of values and spirituality is one of our primary obligations. Some parents, in a misguided effort to extend choice to their children, refuse to teach values during the first eighteen years, preferring that their children reach maturity and select moral beliefs for themselves. Unfortunately, life does not work that way. Children do not live in a vacuum and will select and internalize values from their environment in an attempt to make sense of their world—whether the values are good or bad. In the absence of parental instruction, children become vulnerable to many other influences, and such random selection is not in their favor in today's world.

Gordon B. Hinckley expressed his concern that we spiritually prepare our children when he said: "Each day we are made increasingly aware of the fact that life is more than science and mathematics, more than history and literature. There is a need for another education, without which the substance of our secular learning may lead only to our destruction. I refer to the education of the heart, of the conscience, of the character, of the spirit, these indefinable aspects of our personalities which determine so certainly what we are and what we do in our relationships one with another."[8]

We may feel overwhelmed with the responsibility of our children's moral education, perhaps feeling the need for guidance ourselves. There are many ways of living in the world, and we look for a template to follow. The Lord has asked and answered our most important question: "Therefore, what manner of men ought ye to be? Verily, I say unto you, even as I am" (3 Nephi 27:27). And so we look to see what the Lord is like, that we might pattern our life after Him, and we discover that everything He did was for the good of others. All scripture testifies of His profound love. Never do we see an instance of selfishness. Even when He separated Himself from the clamoring of the multitude, it was for the purpose of worshiping and praying to His Father, thereby strengthening Himself for further service. In His own words, He tells us of His great purpose: "For behold, this is my work and my glory—to bring to pass the immortality and eternal life of man" (Moses 1:39). All He did and suffered was for us.

His great message of love was established when Jesus Christ answered a question regarding the most important of all commandments: "Master, which is the great commandment in the law? Jesus said unto him, Thou shalt love the Lord thy God with all thy heart, and with all thy soul, and with all thy mind. This is the first and great commandment. And the second is like unto it. Thou shalt love thy neighbour as thyself. On these two commandments hang all the law and the prophets" (Matthew 22:36–40). The most basic of all our understandings is that the Lord loves us and we are to follow His divine example and learn to love as well. Love and service to others, then, is our template.

We demonstrate our love for the Lord by serving others. We have been assured that: "Inasmuch as ye have done it unto one of the least of these my brethren, ye have done it unto me" (Matthew 25:40). Other-centeredness, then, is the way we demonstrate the divine-centeredness that is the purpose of our lives. It is the moral compass we use in deciding what we will think about and how we will use our time, and will define for us the spiritual and moral education we need to give to our children.

With such a vision, we see how we, as mothers, need to help our children learn how to be happy in service. This may explain my concern that so many of the activities our children are engaged in today are all about them. We may succeed in teaching them to achieve and to be responsible, but if it is for selfish purposes, have we done them a kindness? We may encourage them to get good grades, but for what purpose? We want them to learn to play the piano, but for what reason? We need to finish these sentences differently. We want them to do well in school so they can contribute, so they can use their talents to build and strengthen and serve. We hope they learn to play the piano so they can bring good music and joy to others and serve in many capacities. We may encourage participation in sports, but why? We realize it will keep them healthy and strong, giving them opportunities to win and lose gracefully, to cooperate with others, to learn responsibility, and to practice being on task and on time. Children need to know that such activities serve to bring balance to their lives. Yet again, we must ask this question: why does that matter? The answer is that when the needs for relaxation and play and socializing are met, and they are educated and prepared, they will be better able to serve. We want our children to have fun, experience joy, and be successful, but they are out-of-balance when their goals and activities are primarily self-centered ones.

There are many ways to serve and in many of the journals and interviews provided to me by the women in my research projects, I witnessed a variety of excellent methods for teaching children to focus on the needs of others. Some undertook humanitarian projects needed to help people of other lands. Others contributed locally. One family met each Sunday in a family council and decided what form their service would assume in the coming week.

In our family, service occurred where we found a need. Corrin was frequently marshalling the forces to help out somewhere, and he never seemed to run out of ideas. If individuals in our circle of awareness did not need anything at the time, there were other worthy projects, such as cleaning the streets or vacant lots to help the community at large. I had to smile when a newly-married daughter confided to me that after two visits to our home with her new husband unprepared for the current service project, he had learned to pack his work clothes. That's great.

Worthy and necessary service projects are a wonderful way to provide meaningful work for children, and for all of us.

Helping young people to catch the vision of a service project is not always easy to do, and sometimes they get it only when they are part way through the experience. We coax our Young Men and Young Women groups to spend some time serving in a nursing home with the promise of basketball and hot chocolate afterwards. They approach the activity unmotivated, but many times in the process of looking to the needs of someone else their feelings change. They are no longer focused on themselves, rather on someone else, and by the time the evening is over they are happy. If we can teach our children to really consider the needs of another person, and get beyond their own self-interest, they will feel the rewards of service.

Learning to become other-centered is a lifelong process and we need to be patient with our children and ourselves. Not long ago, when we were down to three teenagers at home, Corrin and I decided to "kidnap" them and take them on an adventure. So, one Saturday we woke them up fairly early in the morning (quite cheerfully but with some insistence) and asked them to please dress and be in the car in ten minutes. Their responses went something like this: "Oh, I'm so tired." "I just want to sleep." "Why do we have to get up so early?" We assured them they didn't have to go to too much trouble; just be sure they had their athletic shoes on and a warm coat. "Oh, no. It's a service project!" "Why do we have to do one today?" We just smiled and gently urged them on.

They were quite surprised when we got underway and I reached under the seat for some breakfast munchies I had stowed there, and we headed for the North Rim of the Grand Canyon, where we spent a superb day together, enjoying one another and the breathtaking vistas of one of the wonders of the world. I tell you this little story as a reminder that in this lifelong quest to be other-centered, balancing family service projects with purely fun activities will help children to enjoy both work and play more than they would otherwise.

In addition to structured service projects, such as the time we peeled apples for days to support the ward apple butter venture, opportunities to serve others occurred often within the family itself. Many times the children would work hard to plan and carry out a surprise evening for Corrin and me. Since we did not have the means to celebrate our anniversary, or such events as Valentine's Day by going out, the children would create a restaurant on the premises. Candlelit dinners were carefully prepared, usually with menus, waiters, and multiple courses. Once again, it was more than delicious food being served; it was love.

Even though there were plenty of rough spots as the children learned to get along with one another (particularly in tight quarters like the backseat of the car), I could never begin to recount the times when they helped or looked out for one another. From assisting in making posters for the brother or sister running for school office, to purchasing something another person needed but had no way to buy, they supported and served their siblings and their parents.

I remember once responding to some commotion I could hear outside the front door. There was my little five-year-old son protecting his sister, two years younger, from a snarling dog. I could see he was very frightened, but he had placed himself between the dog and his sister and was yelling, "Run, Lana, run." I knew no matter how scared he was he would never leave her. That is being other-centered.

An example which occurred some years later comes to mind. One of my teenage daughters found out that her younger brother had been harassed on the bus. I had to talk her out of taking the matter into her own hands and confronting a group which far outnumbered her. She was thinking only of protecting her brother; there was nothing about her own safety or well-being that concerned her. I witnessed many examples, large and small, of such service and caring among the kids. Even now, the children, both married and single, make it a priority to know how things are going for their brothers and sisters and stand ready to support them if there are any needs.

Does all this service bring happiness? I think it is some measure of success that the children still look for opportunities to be around one another, and they spend a lot of time laughing, playing, visiting, or working together. As our children mature into adults, we deal with conflict, misunderstandings, and irritations. Our children are learning how to behave around others, how to nurture relationships, and how to forgive. We should do all we can to help them do these things as we, too, continue to learn how to nurture and forgive.

As we speak in detail about other-centeredness, we must not lose sight of the higher law. Much has been said in these pages about the sacred stewardship we mothers accept. We nurture our children, worry over them, and give of ourselves to make their lives better. Nevertheless, we must always remember that the other-centeredness we strive to emulate is the second great commandment in the law. The first, and greatest commandment, is to love the Lord with all our heart, might, mind, and soul (see Matthew 22:37–38). It is possible to put another person's welfare ahead of our own, thereby qualifying us as being other-centered, and still not have the Lord first in our thoughts and in our hearts.

We must exercise great caution that we not displace the Lord in our enthusiasm for the welfare of one of His children. I am concerned when

I see mothers so centered upon their children they appear almost to worship them, and we see as a result, neglected husbands and women whose lives are out of balance. This is an unhealthy place to be for both the mother and the child. The Lord has told us, "He that loveth father or mother more than me is not worthy of me: and he that loveth son or daughter more than me is not worthy of me" (Matthew 10:37).

What may cause a mother to lose her perspective? As previously noted, she may have not yet acquired the vision of true mothering and, therefore, this is still about her. If she harbors doubts about the worth of her calling, she may seek to find validation through her children. She needs them to perform well in order to prove to others that she is doing a good job, is using her time well, and still matters for something. Other mothers may have unfulfilled dreams which they transfer to their children, hoping to find vicarious fulfillment as their children accomplish the dreams they once desired for themselves.

Certainly many well-meaning mothers spend an inordinate amount of time pushing and prodding their children toward visible achievement, in the mistaken idea that such observable accomplishments will improve a child's self-esteem. We see a mother spending countless hours working on a son's Eagle Scout project, with or without much interest on the part of the son, to ensure he receives that honor; or we see her preparing a daughter to run for a class office or to compete in a contest.

Unfortunately, such accolades do not necessarily translate into a good self-concept. As we have previously mentioned, children will feel good about themselves when they are willing and able to make a positive difference in the world. This requires genuine skills and a mature desire to contribute in a meaningful way. For this reason, it is imperative that we teach our young people to go for the substance and not for the fluff. It will make little difference to the self-esteem of a young man when he becomes an Eagle Scout if he has been handed merit badges simply because he was a warm body at the scouting activities and had a mother who carried much of the load. The scouting program, at its best, provides leadership training and much useful knowledge and relevant skills. What gives a scouter confidence and capability is the actual learning of the lessons being taught. It's the substance that counts.

Let me give you an example of how aspiring to the plaudits of others can be a negative. I was never a fan of beauty pageants and contests; they seem to be lose-lose propositions. For the girl who wins and is crowned princess or queen, she now shoulders the burden of wondering if she is better than everyone else; others have voted that she is the best. That can be confusing. She may believe them and suffer from that mistaken idea. For the other contestants, they are now losers. What if they believe that appellation at some level? I hoped my daughters would not feel the draw of such contests, but when one or another of them made the decision to compete, I accepted her agency and worked to support her, hoping to make the experience a good one. At the same time, the two of us (and any of my other interested daughters within earshot) had a number of conversations about winning and losing and the true worth of people. Though there are merits to such competitions, such as the opportunity to gain poise and confidence, the risks attendant to such pursuits likely outweigh the possible gains. Poise and confidence can be achieved in other ways without using unconstructive comparisons.

Our sons and daughters need to be made aware of their motivations when they contemplate aspirations and goals. If we are to guide them in this self-knowledge we need to be clear about these matters ourselves. If we seek for the notice or plaudits of others, either for ourselves or for our children, our actions will speak louder than our words. We need to overcome the temptation to bask in reflected glory, and do what is right for the child.

Suppose a teenage daughter is considering whether to accept the opportunity of being head cheerleader at school, and she and her mother discuss the pros and cons of holding that position. The acceptance of this invitation would assure the daughter's popularity, and the mother's pride, but those are not worthy motives since they are entirely self-focused. Also, being head cheerleader would allow the daughter to have fun, to stay in good physical shape, and be part of a team effort. These are better reasons, but still not quite the heart of the matter. What would holding this position mean for others? Would the influence that comes with a title of considerable status be used to exclude others, making the in-crowd even more elite? Or could that same influence be used to reach out, to include and lift others?

The adoration some mothers feel for their children can work to confuse and weaken the children. As mothers, we need to refrain from giving our children a false sense of their own importance. When we continually tell a child that he is "special," the meaning can be unclear. If we mean that the personality, talents, and gifts of any individual child are unique, that would be a true statement. If, however, we believe a child's uniqueness makes him better than others, we tread on shaky ground. If we really believe our son or daughter is special in that sense, we would have to ask and answer this question: as compared to whom?

Do we really want our children to begin judging others and making comparisons? What if we succeed in making them feel they are of more value than another child? We will have burdened them with an untruth, since we know that the Lord loves us all and is no respecter of persons. Mothers would be wise to teach their children that judgment is not based upon the gifts, talents, or sets of circumstances a specific individual has, but, rather, how she serves others with what she has been given. The Lord loves all His children, and we all have worth. As we love the Lord with all our hearts, keeping the greatest of all commandments, we will seek to love His children as He loves them, thereby obeying the second great commandment.

We do not diminish the eminence of the family when we broaden the scope of our love and concern. It is the divine will of the Father that we experience the sweet and tender ties that bind us together as families. Through the eternities yet to come these cherished relationships will fill us with joy. Nevertheless, as we seek to lift and bless the lives of others, and teach our children to do the same, we will come closer to becoming like our Father in Heaven. By precept and example we teach our children to strengthen their peers by including rather than excluding, by lifting rather than putting down, by joining together rather than competing, by teaching rather than judging, and by serving rather than using.

This may seem like a tall order, but it happens daily in small ways: the paper boy who is thanked for his good service; the neighbor playmates who are given more than their share of cookies; the classmate who is chosen first for a ball game, even though her playing skills are poor; the prom attendee who is able to borrow a much-needed dress, and gets a free hairdo thrown in; the friend who is forgiven for forgetting a commitment; the student down the street who is given a last-minute tutorial for an upcoming test. Children are sensitive to our attitudes about others. Through this broadened other-centeredness we show our children how to truly love the Lord. Our children and our families mean more to us than life itself, but we worship the Master.

As we learn to be other-centered and focus on the well-being of others, we will naturally take upon ourselves the timeless virtues taught through the ages. We will be compassionate, tolerant, generous, kind, loyal, and merciful. Those who associate with us can count on us to be honest, truthful, courageous, and full of integrity. Our actions will derive from pure intent and we will do the right thing in the moment.

However, we need to be gentle with ourselves and with our children as we follow the example of the Master. To forget ourselves in service to others is the ultimate goal, yet it will take time to achieve. Though we are commanded by the Lord, "Therefore I would that ye should be perfect even as I, or your Father who is in heaven is perfect," (3 Nephi 12:48) we realize it is an eternal goal and we will never attain perfection in this life. The Lord understands our deficiencies and imperfections and requires only that we do our best. Through His great atoning sacrifice, the Lord will make up the difference after all we can do.

What a comfort that brings to us. Yet, we cannot forget that what we give must truly be the best we can offer. We should make every effort to approximate the divine to the best of our abilities. It is the purpose of this work to identify the eternal principles of mothering in an effort to help us mirror the ideal, without comparing ourselves to others, and without becoming weighed down with guilt or feelings of defeat. When we acquire the vision of mothering as it should be, we can use it as a template for our own mothering.

Notes

1. Jeffrey R. Holland, "The Tongue of Angels," *Ensign*, May 2007, 17.
2. Ezra Taft Benson, "Salvation—A Family Affair," *Ensign*, Jul., 1992, 2.
3. M. Russell Ballard, "Let Our Voices Be Heard," *Liahona*, November, 2003, 16–19, (emphasis his).
4. Gordon B. Hinckley, "Four B's for Boys," *Ensign*, Nov. 1981, 40.
5. *Discourses of Brigham Young*, sel. John A. Widtsoe, (Salt Lake City: Deseret Book, 1946), 207.
6. Gordon B. Hinckley, "The Environment of Our Homes," *Ensign*, June 1985, 6.
7. James E. Faust, "A Thousand Threads of Love," *Ensign*, Oct. 2005, 2–7.
8. Gordon B. Hinckley, Conference Report, Oct. 1964, 116.

Chapter Five

AFTER ALL

After all the heartache and the tears, the hard work and the worry, the wonder and the joys, what can we surmise about mothering? I would hope that we know our course—where we are headed. We should know that mothering is eternal; even if we are unable to have children in this world, it will be our blessing eventually. We know that it is part of the divine design of our Father in Heaven for His children. We understand the principles of mothering that will bring us closer to the ideal. We also know that none of us will get it perfect in this life, and that we do not need to.

Even with these precious truths in our minds and hearts, it takes time and experience to live these principles. Learning to think of others, rather than ourselves, is not easy. Though mothering gives us an unparalleled opportunity for service, there is no magic mantle that descends over us as soon as our first baby is born. We are not immediately transformed. One of the unexpected themes that emerged from the data I analyzed for my dissertation was a finding I characterized as a "growing-into-motherhood phenomenon."[1] I would like to illustrate this phenomenon by using some of the actual responses given by women participating in the research.

A recurring theme mentioned by the women I interviewed dealt with the surprise and sometimes dismay they felt as they first became mothers. Lacey put it this way: "I pictured it as the little white picket fence and the clean kids and the clean house. I think kids get dirtier than I expected. Houses do too." Nicole acknowledged the unrelenting demands of mothering: "I would say it is as busy as about any job could be. It can be high pressure. It can be stressful. . . . It never leaves you. It's always there. Continually. Twenty-four hours a day." Gina agreed, "No one ever explains to you that your whole day is spent working hard. . . . I don't think it was anything I expected." Gayle commented, "To be happy at home is a huge challenge. I decided when I had my first baby I would do it, but it's taken me years to be happy. . . . I think I expected it to be easier. No, it's not what I expected. I thought it would automatically be easy and fulfilling, that I would just flow, and I would just be the gracious, natural mother." Kimberly summarizes the feelings of many young mothers: "[I]t used to be frustrating. When my two little ones were tiny, I just thought, this isn't what I thought Motherhood would be. This is so, I don't know, time consuming. I didn't know it would be so demanding . . . all the physical needs that you have to meet. I just kind of had to grow into Motherhood. Because it came as a big shock. I didn't love it from day one. I mean I didn't just go, oh, this is so wonderful. I thought, oh my word! My life has just changed."[2]

Most of the mothers changed their attitudes and perceptions over time as they adjusted to the mothering role, as the following excerpt from Claudia demonstrates: "It's certainly not glamorous, and . . . it's more work than what I expected it to be . . . but you know . . . I've noticed especially as my kids get a little older, it is more fun. It is fun. And you know, having little babies . . . it was a little harder I think, and where my kids are getting a little older, I've really enjoyed it."[3]

We see how Claudia changes her view of mothering as time passes. This growing positive response to mothering was a frequent finding among the women. The women became happier in their mothering role. They, themselves, ascribed their changing attitudes to the external circumstances in their lives. They saw their constrained social networks and finances, as well as the heavy demands related to the care of infants, as being the factors that made their early mothering experiences more difficult. Because the women who participated in this research were blind as to the purposes of the study (so as to provide unbiased responses), they did not consider that their early discontent might be due to their focus being more on themselves during these early years, rather than being on their children. It was clear in the research, that over time the mothers began to think more about the welfare of their children, and less about their own interests.

After studying the data, these are the conclusions I drew:

It is feasible that a change in focus took place as these women shifted their attention from themselves to the ones they cared for, and ultimate goals were more carefully considered and applied. As evidence for such a supposition several factors need to be measured.

First, for some of the women the external circumstances of their lives have not improved. Financial worries and inadequate housing problems are still affecting them. For others there are still long days and sleepless nights with newborns. In practical terms the increase in responsibility and work increased dramatically as their families grew in size and diversity, and as they added substantial church and community obligations they had not formerly held.

Second, and most importantly, the time in their lives just previous to becoming brides and mothers was a time when they were more likely to be focused on their own goals and needs. They had no intimate others they were responsible for. They speak of the things they did prior to marriage and mention holding down jobs, going to school (some are college graduates), and traveling. From this single status they moved rapidly into a position where they must now think of someone else before they think of themselves. They no longer have paychecks, perks, and recognition.

There are probably many variables which play into the improving attitude regarding the role of mothering that we see in the participants. Included among those might be the additional help and companionship that older children in the home provide, the increased capability and confidence to help that comes with practice, etc. However, the focus-of-attention theory may also illuminate the grow-into-motherhood phenomenon. In the journal writings the women wrote continuously about their children: what they were doing, what their needs were, how much they admired them, or enjoyed watching them, or worried over them. This contrasts with the accounts they gave of new motherhood. Perhaps their anxiety about their own needs grew less as they became more concerned with the needs of their children. The mental tally they kept of the costs of care-giving was set aside, as they realized there was something that was ultimately more important to them, and they began to get their enjoyment from making the lives better for the ones they loved. Essentially, their focus changed.[4]

It is well for us to remember, as we consider the "change in perspective" required of new mothers, that our society does not prepare young women to abruptly transform their lives when they marry. Our daughters are encouraged to be well-educated, to be capable of making a living, and to strive for excellence as they learn and grow—just as our sons are. They are encouraged to prepare for careers and to prepare for making contributions in their fields of interest. For our sons, the trajectory they began when they were young continues throughout their lives. For our daughters, however, their underlying purpose seems to alter when they become mothers, and they may feel a resulting disconnect. In reality, the elemental purpose of a woman should not change partway through life. The trajectory should remain constant, just as it does for a man.

In order for this constancy to happen, we must help our girls look forward to the challenges and joys of rearing wonderful families. This should be the heart of their preparation. If we are not careful to make the vision of mothering real and valued for our young women, the adjustment required when they change direction midstream will continue to plague them. Education should continue to be a paramount goal for both our girls and boys. Nevertheless, the reasons for being educated differ. Our young men need to prepare to provide for a family. Our young women need to be educated, articulate, capable women and mothers, who are able to nurture children and center the family in a constructive and fulfilling way. They should also be able to provide financial support if that should be required, and to contribute to society when time and family circumstances permit. Both sons and daughters need the fulfillment, joy, awareness, and competence education can give them.

What if a mother comprehends the vision, but feels that motherhood demands more than she is capable of giving? What if it all seems just too much? It is sobering when we recognize the serious consequences attendant to how we handle our responsibilities, especially when we realize our interactions with our children have lifelong, even eternal, implications. Allow me to suggest four ways mothers can reach out for help in meeting this divine commitment.

First, one of the ways mothers can gain the skills necessary to be an effective mother is to become well-educated. We have previously spoken of the importance of secular learning, but the subject bears repeating in the present framework. We may need to sift out the chaff, but there are many kernels of information which can make us better and more confident in our mothering. Let me illustrate with a few examples.

We know that most teenagers are self-conscious about how they look, and may spend hours in front of a mirror. This self-inspection is a normal part of the teenage experience in our culture. Suppose your fifteen-year-old son (the age for males when body image is at its lowest point), thinks he is the world's worst specimen. He feels like his legs are everywhere they shouldn't be, and his face appears to him to be growing homelier by the minute. It is helpful if we can reassure him, that legs, feet, hands, and arms grow faster than does the trunk of the body, and that ears and noses grow faster than the overall size of the head. His confidence will improve when we can inform him that the day will come when all his body parts will catch up with one another and he will be a well-proportioned young man. Knowing some important facts about physical development, such as the uneven growth experienced during adolescence, can help mothers guide children through the physical changes they will experience.

Knowing the development of cognitive or mental processing is helpful in the same way. In order to understand algebra, an individual must attain a level of cognitive maturation which allows her to do certain mental operations, such as abstract reasoning. There are many people who go through life hating mathematics because they were expected to do something they were not ready for developmentally. That is a helpful piece of information to understand.

Even knowledge concerning psychosocial development can make parenting easier. A mother may worry unnecessarily if Susie, her usually happy and gregarious eight-month-old daughter, cries and fusses when Aunt Molly and Uncle Jack try to hold her. If the mother is aware that "stranger anxiety" is common in children of that age, she may feel more relaxed about the situation, and calmly protect Susie's security by not forcing her into the arms of strangers. The mother knows from her studies that a three-month-old infant will often happily go to any smiling face, whereas older babies may be less comfortable meeting new people. These older babies have matured enough to recognize when someone new has entered their world, and therefore, their tolerance for new faces may become an issue. Secular learning deserves a definite place in our schooling as we learn the art and science of good mothering.

The second way a mother can reach out for help is to recognize and use eternal principles and divine modeling in her stewardship. This, too, is a resource we have spoken of previously. It is a higher source of help and instruction than the secular learning we just described because it provides us with the lens through which we may identify which secular ideas and practices are worthy of emulation. If we are concerned about the behavior of one of our children and desire to correct or improve it, we should be careful that our intervention meets the requirements of the timeless principles given to us by the Lord. Elder Boyd K. Packer said, "True doctrine, understood, changes attitudes and behavior. The study of the doctrines of the gospel will improve behavior quicker than a study of behavior will improve behavior."[5] This is our surest source of insight; the gospel truths are given to us to learn and apply, and help is just a prayer away.

The third way we can learn how to be good mothers is one which we have not discussed previously. It consists of carefully observing and modeling other mothers—a traditional method used for thousands of years. Much wisdom has been garnered through the centuries which we would be well-served to make our own. We have generally been reared by our own mothers and have watched the ways they have loved us, kept us safe, and trained us. As we live alongside our mothers, we serve a kind of apprenticeship, and repeat in our own homes many of the behaviors we saw modeled in the homes of our childhood, both good and bad.

We need to be discriminating as we consider the actions of our own and other mothers, and realize we will be empowered if we add to such inherited wisdom, the secular learning, and divine principles spoken of above. Since circumstances do change from generation to generation, the challenges mothers face change as well, and we must fall back on time-proven principles as our reliable guides. For example, on the very serious issue of pornography, it was easier for me to protect my children from its pernicious influence than it is today, where now it is but a few clicks away.

The fourth point I would like to address, regarding sources a mother may turn to for help, is another one we have not yet addressed, and concerns the assistance she may receive from her husband. It is much easier for a woman to embrace her stewardship with capacity and joy, if her husband is fulfilling his own stewardship well. Along with all the counsel given to mothers, fathers should be accountable as well. The burden on a mother becomes an unfair one if her companion does not preside, provide, and protect as he has been instructed. Though this is not a work about fathers, the integral part he plays in the family needs to be considered.

I recalled the results of my master's thesis as I contemplated the role of the husband. My research was designed to see how being other-centered correlated with being depressed (or happy) among LDS mothers. In order to isolate the effect of other-centeredness, it was necessary to control and account for other variables which may affect a mother's happiness, such as health, education, number of children, socioeconomic status, age, or the relationship she has with her husband. Therefore, I gathered data on those variables as well. There were 183 LDS mothers who participated in the study. Of interest in the present context was the fact that, though I found a statistically significant inverse correlation between other-centeredness and depression, the relationship with the husband accounted for the greatest amount of the variance. In simple terms, the relationship with the husband was the strongest predictor of depression.[6]

Because my thesis is a secular, scientifically-based work, the interpretation of the data has to be contained within prescribed parameters. I was looking to see how other-centeredness and depression occur together. When the level of other-centeredness varies, will the level of depression vary as well? In a correlation design we cannot assume causality. I found that as other-centeredness increased, depression decreased, and thereby confirmed a correlational reality, but for scientific rigor I am not permitted to make the assumption that being other-centered causes a person to be happy. It is possible that happy people tend to be other-centered. Therefore, I reported this conclusion in my thesis: "It may well be that those women who have a poor relationship with their husband may have a difficult time being other-centered. Or perhaps, those who are other-centered are better able to nurture a positive relationship with their husband."[7]

In the present work, however, we are not limited in our interpretations and can add the light of the gospel to illuminate our understanding. We know that as we lose our lives in the service of others, we will be happy, and those "others" of which we speak can be children or husbands. Just as we strive to do the right thing for the child, we try to do what is best for the husband. The same cautions we use with children apply to husbands as well. To permit a husband to ignore, belittle, or mistreat us is not in his best interest. If we allow him to use us as a doormat, someday he will need to make an accounting of that behavior. It is kinder to him if we require him to respect us and treat us well. Kindness is always a necessary ingredient in a successful marital relationship, and as we love and serve our companion, and put his needs ahead of our own, we will be rewarded. He may not choose to respond to our best efforts, but in such instances we must acknowledge his gift of agency, while still preserving our integrity by doing the right thing.

Certainly, a caring, supportive husband who shares the vision of great mothering and eternal families is of inestimable worth. I have such a husband, and can attest to this personally. Nevertheless, it must be pointed out that mothers who do not have such a committed husband, or perhaps have no husband at all, can still be the great mothers it is their birthright to be. It is just much, much more difficult. We cannot always change our environment, but our Heavenly Father knows under what restrictive circumstances we labor, and will guide and assist us in our work.

One of the most interesting results of my master's research project was this finding: out of the 183 participants in the study, the 19 women who scored the highest on the other-centeredness scale suffered from no depression whatsoever. It is possible, of course, that mothers who reached this apex of other-centeredness and happiness were able to achieve this ideal because they experienced no significant problems or issues in their life with regard to their relationship with their husband, their age, wealth, education, or health. It is more likely, however, that these particular women had challenges common to all of us, but had grasped the vision of other-centeredness in such a way they were able to transcend personal circumstances and focus on the needs of others. Mothers can face almost unimaginable challenges and still triumph. The Lord wants us to be successful.

As the divine design becomes clearer to us, we begin to understand how to be great mothers. We learn how to parent by looking at how our Heavenly Father parents. By following the patterns that He has given us, we refine our homes. We are predictable, because our Father in Heaven is the same yesterday, today, and tomorrow. We are accessible, because help for us is only a prayer away. We teach our children to have order, because we know our Father's house is a house of order. We teach our children to work, to be obedient, to learn, and to take responsibility for the same reason—our Father expects the same of us. And we learn to do all we do with love. The Savior instructed us, "A new commandment I give unto you, That ye love one another; as I have loved you, that ye also love one another" (John 13:34). The Lord loves us purely and with a desire to do what is right for us. When we purely love our children, we will want what is right for them. Paul reminds us, "Love worketh no ill to his neighbor; therefore love is the fulfilling of the law" (Romans 13:10). It always has to be the right thing.

Near the beginning of the Book of Mormon, Nephi tells us the fundamental reason for leaving a written record of his day: "For the fulness of mine intent is that I may persuade men to come unto the God of Isaac, and the God of Jacob, and be saved" (1 Nephi 6:4). He explains further what he is not about doing: "Wherefore, the things which are pleasing unto the world I do not write, but the things which are pleasing unto God and unto those who are not of the world" (1 Nephi 6:5). In a similar vein, I paused frequently as I wrote this book to review my intent. My desire was and is to bring reverent attention to the divine mission of mothering and to renew our vision of how we can draw nearer to that ideal. Like Nephi, I chose not to write what is pleasing unto the world. Indeed, the thoughts within these pages are frequently in striking contrast to what the world espouses. Instead, this book is written to those who are in this world but "who are not of the world," as Nephi envisioned them.

I have often asked myself why I decided to write about values which are no longer popular in our society. I am speaking of other-centeredness in a world full of self-focusing images. We are taught to look out for number one, to consider our own needs and expectations, to examine the cost/benefit ratio of our every action. We are conditioned to ask, what's in it for me? With this increasing selfishness the role of women has been under attack. President N. Eldon Tanner expressed it this way: "It is of great concern to all who understand this glorious concept that Satan and his cohorts are using scientific arguments and nefarious propaganda to lure women away from their primary responsibilities as wives, mothers, and homemakers. We hear so much about emancipation, independence, sexual liberation, birth control, abortion, and other insidious propaganda belittling the role of motherhood, all of which is Satan's way of destroying women, the home, and the family—the basic unit of society."[8]

This trend toward redefining the roles of women in an effort to change or dilute their divine meaning is undermining the well-being of our children, and that is my concern and reason for writing. Mothering cannot be "fitted in" around other priorities—either society's or our own. Because I have a testimony this is true, I cannot be silent. Selfishly, I would rather write the "in thing" or what is politically and socially correct, or perhaps be safe and write nothing at all, but that is not an option. We read in 2 Nephi 8:7, "Hearken unto me, ye that know righteousness, the people in whose heart I have written my law, fear not the reproach of men, neither be ye afraid of their revilings." The truths I know about mothering have been written in my heart. They cannot be denied, no matter how unpopular they may be. We are told to experiment upon the words of the Lord (see

Alma 32). I gained my testimony about mothering by exercising faith that the Lord knows best how children should be reared. We can each know the authenticity of these eternal principles by living them and finding out for ourselves. My search through the years to find "what makes a person happy" never was satisfied by studying the theories of men. There surely are truths and pieces of the puzzle which insightful men and women have contributed to the understanding we have of ourselves, and of our life experiences. Yet only the gospel in its simplicity has the resolution to our dilemmas and uncertainties. Love is our answer. Living the two great commandments, to love the Lord and to love our neighbor, in the best sense of which we are capable, is the way to happiness—for us and for our children. There is no other way.

As I bring this book to a close, I cannot help wondering what my children will think of it. When I mentioned to one of my sons that I was contemplating writing a work such as this, he reminded me that the children may have different perspectives from the ones I have. That gave me pause, and I realized that what he said was true. Nevertheless, my purpose is to write from the perspective of a mother—which is the only perspective I have. So, though my memory may not be perfect as to every detail, this is a true story of mothering.

For each of us as mothers, we have to become comfortable with our imperfect mothering. We make mistakes—many of them over time. If I could do it all again knowing what I know now, I'm sure I would do better; but I would still make mistakes. Our married children are currently in the process of making their own mistakes—though they will hopefully be fewer. Each generation should be better and build on the last, and I see many things these new parents are doing that I wish we had done or done better than we did. Their home evenings and family scripture-study routines seem to have fewer interruptions than ours did, and they see to it that a father's priesthood blessing is given to each school-age child at the beginning of every school year. I wish we had done that. Our children will have to learn to forgive us, as we forgave them so many times when we tucked them into bed, after a day of putting up with their antics and their demands.

I am especially glad that the opportunity of being a mother is an eternal one, even though the experience of being a mother can be bittersweet. Our hearts ache for our children at times, and mothers are not magic and able to fix things in a blink of an eye. Just this morning I received a phone call from one of my children who was worried that the stress one of her siblings was experiencing was serious enough that it was becoming a health concern. And, I wondered what I could do in a situation where there were no easy fixes. If only they were small again and I could bandage a knee or pull them onto my lap. There will always be challenges for each of us, and sometimes what we can do to help seems inadequate. In such instances, we must leave it in the hands of the Lord—always remembering the remarkable and fulfilling times we as mothers have been blessed to have, and being grateful for that incomparable opportunity.

Knowing I can be a mother forever makes it easier to manage the adjustments that come with the changing seasons of life. If I were granted my selfish, personal preferences, I would always have my children around me, even though I know they need to move forward into their own futures and families. Sometimes I am happy that four of them are still single so I feel more a part of their lives, and yet I pray every day that they will in due time find someone they can be happily married to, and will move forward by rearing families of their own. And when the last one marries, I will feel a little sad in the midst of the celebrating, but I will let him or her go. After all, I am a mother . . . and I must do what is right for the child.

Notes

1. Janice G. Nielson, "A Descriptive Study of the Experience of Helping in the Lives of Latter-day Saint Women" (dissertation, Brigham Young University, Dec. 1999), 131–5.
2. Ibid.
3. Ibid.
4. Ibid.
5. Boyd K. Packer, "Little Children," *Ensign*, Nov. 1986, 17.
6. Janice G. Nielson, "Other Centeredness and Depression in a Sample of Mormon Women," (master's thesis, Brigham Young University, Aug. 1994).
7. Ibid, p. 44
8. N. Eldon Tanner, "No Greater Honor: The Woman's Role," *Ensign*, Jan. 1974, 7

About the Author

Janice Gerber Nielson grew up in Provo, Utah. She and her husband, Corrin, reared a large family of eleven children in southern Utah. She received her BS degree at Southern Utah State College (now Southern Utah University) and her MS and PhD from Brigham Young University in psychology, with a special interest in mothering and developmental issues. She has taught at Dixie State College and Brigham Young University. She and her husband recently spent several years teaching university students in China and now reside in northern Utah.

You may visit her at her website: www.janicenielson.com.